PREFACE

1. Scope

This publication provides overarching doctrine for special operations and the employment and support of special operations forces across the range of military operations.

2. Purpose

This publication has been prepared under the direction of the Chairman of the Joint Chiefs of Staff. It sets forth joint doctrine to govern the activities and performance of the Armed Forces of the United States in joint operations and provides the doctrinal basis for interagency coordination and for US military involvement in multinational operations. It provides military guidance for the exercise of authority by combatant commanders and other joint force commanders (JFCs) and prescribes joint doctrine for operations, education, and training. It provides military guidance for use by the Armed Forces in preparing their appropriate plans. It is not the intent of this publication to restrict the authority of the JFC from organizing the force and executing the mission in a manner the JFC deems most appropriate to ensure unity of effort in the accomplishment of the overall objective.

3. Application

a. Joint doctrine established in this publication apply to the Joint Staff, commanders of combatant commands, subordinate unified commands, joint task forces, subordinate components of these commands, and the Services.

b. The guidance in this publication is authoritative; as such, this doctrine will be followed except when, in the judgment of the commander, exceptional circumstances dictate otherwise. If conflicts arise between the contents of this publication and the contents of Service publications, this publication will take precedence unless the Chairman of the Joint Chiefs of Staff, normally in coordination with the other members of the Joint Chiefs of Staff, has provided more current and specific guidance. Commanders of forces operating as part of a multinational (alliance or coalition) military command should follow multinational doctrine and procedures ratified by the United States. For doctrine and procedures not ratified by the United States, commanders should evaluate and follow the multinational command's doctrine and procedures, where applicable and consistent with US law, regulations, and doctrine.

For the Chairman of the Joint Chiefs of Staff:

WILLIAM E. GORTNEY
Vice Admiral, USN
Director, Joint Staff

Intentionally Blank

UNITED STATES SPECIAL OPERATIONS COMMAND
OFFICE OF THE COMMANDER
7701 TAMPA POINT BOULEVARD
MACDILL AIR FORCE BASE, FLORIDA 33621-5323

Joint Publication (JP) 3-05 *Joint Special Operations* is the culmination of a major collaborative effort within the joint community. This publication has captured our best characterization yet of the functions, organization, employment, and synchronization of Special Operations Forces (SOF).

USSOCOM is responsible for the development of special operations doctrine as assigned in US Code, Title 10, and DoD Directive 5100.01. JP 3-05 and the five other joint publications for which USSOCOM is designated as the lead agent are fundamental to this effort. USSOCOM is also developing SOF-specific doctrine, mirroring the responsibilities of the military departments to develop service-specific doctrine.

Joint Special Operations doctrine provides the foundation for common understanding of key terms and concepts that help SOF work effectively with the joint force, partner nations, and other stakeholder agencies. While recognizing that no published doctrine exactly matches operational circumstances, this document is provided as a primary reference to guide the Joint Force Commander's employment of SOF.

ERIC T. OLSON
Admiral, U.S. Navy

Intentionally Blank

SUMMARY OF CHANGES
REVISION OF JOINT PUBLICATION 3-05, DATED 17 DECEMBER 2003

- Subsumes sections of special operations and the principles of war, special operations and the principles of military operations other than war, and the nature of special operations into one discussion of special operations across the range of military operations.

- Discusses the following as part of command and control of special operations forces (SOF): SOF as the lead for a joint task force, integration and interoperability of conventional forces and SOF, interorganizational coordination, and multinational coordination.

- Introduces the concept Special Operations Joint Task Force (SOJTF) through which United States Special Operations Command will present all theater SOF under one special operations commander.

- Incorporates a stand-alone section on geospatial information and services support of SOF into a general discussion of support considerations.

- Adds sections on operational contract support, host-nation support, protection, maritime support, information operations support, and multinational support.

- Deletes an appendix on SOF education and training.

- Implements the change from the term "psychological operations" (PSYOP) to "military information support operations" (MISO).

- Revises and updates numerous definitions in accordance with current directives and practice.

- Deletes discussion of SOF truths.

- Reflects the development of a United States Marine Corps SOF capability.

Intentionally Blank

TABLE OF CONTENTS

APPENDIX

GLOSSARY

FIGURES

EXECUTIVE SUMMARY
COMMANDER'S OVERVIEW

- **Provides an Overview of Joint Special Operations**

- **Describes Special Operations Forces and Their Core Activities**

- **Describes Command and Control of Joint Special Operations**

- **Discusses the Support of Joint Special Operations**

Overview of Special Operations

United States Special Operations Command deploys and sustains special operations forces (SOF) to facilitate operations with conventional forces (CF), to promote synergy among all SOF elements, and to provide more efficient command and control (C2) structures.

Special operations (SO) differ from conventional operations in degree of physical and political risk, operational techniques, modes of employment, and dependence on detailed operational intelligence and indigenous assets. SO are conducted in all environments, but are particularly well suited for denied and politically sensitive environments. SO can be tailored to achieve not only military objectives through application of special operations forces (SOF) capabilities for which there are no broad conventional force requirements, but also to support the application of the diplomatic, informational, and economic instruments of national power.

Special Operations and Their Core Activities

Designated SOF

SOF are those forces identified in Title 10, United States Code (USC), Section 167 or those units or forces that have since been designated as SOF by Secretary of Defense (SecDef). Generally, SOF are under the combatant command (command authority) (COCOM) of the Commander, United States Special Operations Command (CDRUSSOCOM), or the respective geographic combatant commander (GCC) to which they are assigned. SOF are those Active Component and Reserve Component forces of the Services specifically organized, trained, and equipped to conduct and support SO.

Characteristics of SOF

SOF are inherently joint. When employed, SOF are presented with their command and control (C2) structure intact, which facilitates their integration into joint force plans, retains cohesion, and provides a control mechanism to address SO specific concerns and coordinate their activities with other components and supporting commands.

SOF are distinct from conventional forces (CF). Most SOF personnel undergo a careful selection process and mission-specific training beyond basic military skills to achieve entry-level SO skills.

SOF Capabilities. SOF can be formed into versatile, self-contained teams that provide a joint force commander (JFC) with a flexible force capable of operating in ambiguous and swiftly changing scenarios.

SOF are not a substitute for CF. In most cases SOF are neither trained, organized, nor equipped to conduct sustained conventional combat operations and, therefore, should not be substituted for CF that are able to effectively execute that mission.

Most SO missions require non-SOF support.

Five SOF Mission Criteria

It must be an appropriate mission or activity for SOF.

The mission or activities should support the JFC's campaign or operation plan, or special activities.

Mission or tasks must be operationally feasible, approved, and fully coordinated.

Required resources must be available to execute and support the SOF mission.

The expected outcome of the mission must justify the risks.

Special Operations Core Activities

SOF are specifically organized, trained, and equipped to accomplish the 11 core activities: direct action, special reconnaissance, counterproliferation of weapons of mass destruction, counterterrorism, unconventional warfare, foreign internal defense, security force assistance, counterinsurgency, information operations (IO), military information support operations (MISO), and civil affairs operations.

Command and Control of Special Operations Forces

C2 of SOF normally should be executed within a SOF chain of command.	**SOF may be assigned to either CDRUSSOCOM or a GCC.** The identification of a C2 organizational structure for SOF should depend upon specific objectives, security requirements, and the operational environment.
Liaison	Liaison among all components of the joint force and SOF, however they are organized, is vital for effective SOF employment, as well as coordination, deconfliction, synchronization, and the prevention of fratricide.
SOF in the United States	Unless otherwise directed by SecDef, all SOF based in the continental United States are assigned to United States Special Operations Command (USSOCOM) and under the COCOM of CDRUSSOCOM. USSOCOM is a unified command (Title 10, USC, Section 167) that has the responsibilities of a functional combatant command and responsibilities similar to a Military Department in areas unique to SO.
SOF in Theater	SOF assigned to a GCC are under the COCOM of the respective GCC. A GCC normally exercises operational control of all assigned and attached SOF through the commander, theater special operations command (CDRTSOC) or a subordinate JFC. The CDRTSOC also may be designated as the joint force special operations component commander (JFSOCC) by the GCC.
Theater Special Operations Command	The theater special operations command (TSOC) is the primary theater SOF organization capable of performing broad continuous missions uniquely suited to SOF capabilities. The TSOC is also the primary mechanism by which a GCC exercises C2 over SOF.
SOF Operational C2	The **JFSOCC** is the commander within a unified command, subordinate unified command, or joint task force (JTF) responsible to the establishing commander for making recommendations on the proper employment of assigned, attached, and/or made available for tasking SOF and assets; planning and coordinating SO; or accomplishing such operational missions as may be assigned. The JFSOCC is given the

authority necessary to accomplish missions and tasks assigned.

A **joint special operations task force (JSOTF)** is a JTF composed of SO units from more than one Service, formed to carry out specific SO or prosecute SO in support of a theater campaign or other operations. A JSOTF may have CF tasked to support the conduct of specific missions.

SOF Subordinate C2 Organizations. A JSOTF, by its joint designation, has SOF from more than one of the Services: Army SOF, Navy SOF, Air Force SOF, or Marine Corps SOF, and these designations typically denote their forces and subordinate units, not a headquarters.

SOF as the Lead for a Joint Task Force

In some cases, a C2 construct based on *SO expertise and influence* may be better suited to the overall conduct of an operation (i.e., superiority in the aggregate of applicable capabilities, experience, specialized equipment, and knowledge of and relationships with relevant populations), with the JTF being built around a core SO staff. Such a JTF has both SOF and CF and the requisite ability to command and control them. SOF and their unique capabilities are particularly well-suited for such complex situations because of their regional familiarity, language and cultural awareness, and understanding of the social dynamics within and among the relevant populations (i.e., tribal politics, social networks, religious influences, and customs and mores).

Such a construct calls for a SOF joint force commander, not as a joint force special operations component commander /commander joint special operations task force, but as the commander, joint task force.

Integration and Interoperability of CF and SOF

Effective SOF-CF integration facilitates the synchronizing of military operations in time, space, and purpose; maximizes the capability of the joint force; allows the JFC to optimize the principles of joint operations in planning and execution; and may produce an operating tempo and battle rhythm with which the enemy is unable to cope. It may also reduce the potential for fratricide. Accordingly, focus should be placed on three key areas: operations, command relationships, and liaisons.

Coordination and Liaison Elements

SOF commanders have specific elements that facilitate liaison and coordination. They include the special operations command and control element (SOCCE) to command and control, and coordinate SOF activities with CF; the special operations liaison element (SOLE) to provide liaison to the joint force air component commander (JFACC) or appropriate Service component air C2 facility; and SOF liaison officers placed in a variety of locations as necessary to coordinate, synchronize, and deconflict SO within the operational area.

Joint Special Operations Area

The **JFC may establish a joint special operations area (JSOA),** which is a restricted area of land, sea, and airspace assigned by a JFC to the commander of a joint SO force to conduct SO activities. When a JSOA is designated, the JFSOCC (or commander, joint special operations task force [CDRJSOTF]) is the supported commander within the designated JSOA.

Interorganizational Coordination

Interagency coordination is as integral to SO as it is conventional operations, and fostering personal relationships between SOF commanders and interorganizational leaders and professional relations between both staffs should be a routine objective during military engagement activities.

Multinational Coordination

SOF operate with multinational forces, i.e., forces belonging to a coalition or alliance, on a routine and recurring basis. US SOF assess, train, advise, assist, and operate with a plethora of multinational foreign SO units.

Support Considerations for Special Operations Forces

SOF support must be tailored to specific mission requirements, yet flexible enough to respond to changing employment parameters.

The joint character of SO requires support arrangements across Service lines with emphasis on unique support required in order to sustain independent and remote operations. Further, SOF must be able to exploit information derived from the full range of available multinational, national, theater, and tactical intelligence, surveillance, and reconnaissance support systems.

Intelligence Support

All-source, fused intelligence is vital in identifying relevant targets, course of action development, and mission planning/execution. SO require detailed planning, often by relatively small units. Consequently, intelligence requirements are normally greater in scope and depth than that of CF. Joint intelligence preparation of the operational environment provides the foundation for SO intelligence production.

Operational Contract Support

The continual introduction of high-tech equipment, coupled with force structure and manning limitations, and high operating tempo mean that SOF may be augmented with contracted support, including contingency contractor employees and all tiers of subcontractor employees who are specifically authorized through their contract to accompany the force and have protected status in accordance with international conventions (i.e., contractors authorized to accompany the force).

Host-Nation Support

Host-nation support (HNS) is that civil and/or military assistance rendered by a nation to foreign forces within its territory based on agreements mutually concluded between nations. For SO, HNS must be weighed against operations security considerations, mission requirements and duration, and the operational environment.

Logistic Support

GCCs and their Service component commanders, in coordination with the CDRTSOC, are responsible for ensuring that effective and responsive support systems are developed and provided for assigned/attached SOF.

Health Service Support

SOF teams frequently operate in remote areas and therefore, are exposed to health threats not normally seen in the other areas of the respective host nations. Point-to-point movement to designated Medical Treatment Facilities is standard while medical regulating and strategic aeromedical evacuation might be required and should be part of the contingency planning process.

Communications Systems Support

Communications systems support to SOF normally are global, secure, and jointly interoperable. It must be flexible so that it can be tailored to specific SO missions and it must add value to the SOF operational capability. SOF must be able to communicate anywhere and anytime using the full range of national capabilities required to support the mission.

Public Affairs Support	The diplomatic and political sensitivity of many SO mandates that thorough and accurate public affairs guidance be developed during the operational planning stage and approved for use in advance of most SO.
Combat Camera Support	Combat camera provides still and video documentary products that support MISO and other SO missions. Many combat camera teams supporting SOF are specially equipped with night vision and digital image transmission capabilities.
Legal Support	SO missions frequently involve a unique set of complex issues. There are federal laws and executive orders, federal agency publications and directives, the law of armed conflict, and rules of engagement that may affect SO missions as well as the SO joint planning and targeting processes.
Protection	Protection focuses on conserving the SOF fighting potential, whether operating independently, or as part of a larger joint force in a major operation/campaign. For force protection, typically each GCC has tactical control of US forces in their area of responsibility.
Fire Support	SOF may require long-range, surface-based, joint fire support in remote locations or for targets well beyond the land, maritime, and amphibious operational force area of operations. SOF liaison elements coordinate fire support through both external and SOF channels. SOF liaison elements (e.g., SOCCE and SOLE) provide SOF expertise to coordinate, synchronize, and deconflict SOF fire support.
Air Support	In addition to their organic air capabilities for infiltration, exfiltration, resupply, and precision fire support, SOF often require conventional air support that requires timely and detailed planning and coordination. Air support is typically provided by the JFACC (or an Air Force component commander), and the JFSOCC/CDRJSOTF normally provides a SOLE to the JFACC at the joint air operations center.
Maritime Support	Maritime support is provided by the joint force maritime component commander, the Navy component commander, and/or the Marine Corps component

commander. Maritime support includes fire support, seabasing operations, deception, and deterrence.

Space Support

Space based support to SOF can include: precision navigation and/or geopositioning, global communications, global intelligence collection, surveillance and warning, meteorological support, imagery for geospatial support and targeting, blue force tracking data, and denying adversary use of space-based capabilities.

Meteorological and Oceanographic Support

This [meteorological and oceanographic support] information can be used by the commander to choose the best windows of opportunity to execute, support, and sustain specific SOF operations.

Cyberspace Support

Cyberspace operations in support of SO can often be conducted remotely, thus reducing the SOF footprint and contributing to freedom of action within a given operational area.

Information Operations Support

IO is a SOF core activity, and also integral to the successful execution of many SO. SO may require support from any combination of core, supporting, or related IO capabilities, so the JFC's IO cell should include a SOF representative.

Multinational Support

Multinational support to SOF complements HNS and depends on mission and capability requirements. Common examples include information and intelligence sharing; providing liaison teams and support to planning efforts; materiel assistance; basing, access, and overflight permission; humanitarian assistance; and linguists and cultural advice and awareness.

CONCLUSION

This publication provides overarching doctrine for SO and the employment and support of SOF across the range of military operations.

CHAPTER I
OVERVIEW OF SPECIAL OPERATIONS

> *"Today we see a bewildering diversity of separatist wars, ethnic and religious violence, coups d'état, border disputes, civil upheavals, and terrorist attacks, pushing waves of poverty-stricken, war-ridden immigrants (and hordes of drug traffickers as well) across national boundaries. In the increasingly wired global economy, many of these seemingly small conflicts trigger strong secondary effects in surrounding (and even distant) countries. Thus a "many small wars" scenario is compelling military planners in many armies to look afresh at what they call "special operations" or "special forces"—the niche warriors of tomorrow."*
>
> **Alvin and Heidi Toffler**
> ***War and Anti-War**, Survival at the Dawn of the 21st Century 1993*

1. Introduction

This publication provides fundamental principles and guidance for the Services, combatant commanders (CCDRs), and subordinate joint force commanders (JFCs) to prepare for and conduct special operations (SO). It describes those military operations and provides general guidance for military commanders to employ and execute command and control (C2) of special operations forces (SOF) assigned/attached to a geographic combatant commander (GCC), subordinate unified commander, or a commander, joint task force (CJTF). Other specific SO operational guidelines are provided in Joint Publication (JP) 3-05.1, *Joint Special Operations Task Force Operations*; JP 3-13.2, *Military Information Support Operations*, JP 3-22, *Foreign Internal Defense,* and JP 3-57, *Civil-Military Operations*. Additionally, SOF maintain core competencies in counterinsurgency (COIN) and counterterrorism (CT) operations that are discussed in detail in JP 3-24, *Counterinsurgency Operations,* and JP 3-26, *Counterterrorism.* This chapter introduces SO, the nature of SO, and how they relate to the principles of joint operations and the range of military operations. Chapter II, "Special Operations Forces and Their Core Activities," focuses on the SOF and particularly the 11 SOF core activities. Chapter III, "Command and Control of Special Operations Forces," discusses C2 and coordination, and Chapter IV, "Support Considerations for Special Operations Forces," outlines numerous support considerations for SOF.

2. Special Operations

SO are conducted in all environments, but are particularly well suited for denied and politically sensitive environments. SO can be tailored to achieve not only military objectives through application of SOF capabilities for which there are no broad conventional force requirements, but also to support the application of the diplomatic, informational, and economic instruments of national power. SO are typically low visibility or clandestine operations. SO are applicable across the range of military operations. They can be conducted independently or in conjunction with operations of conventional forces (CF) or other government agencies (OGAs), or host nations (HNs)/partner nations (PNs), and may include operations with or through indigenous, insurgent, and/or irregular forces. SO differ from conventional operations in degree of physical and political risk, operational techniques, modes of employment, and dependence on detailed operational intelligence and indigenous assets.

a. SO are often conducted at great distances from major operating bases with operating units widely separated in a distributed manner across the operational area(s). SOF employ sophisticated communications systems and special means of infiltration, support, and exfiltration to penetrate and return from hostile, denied, or politically sensitive areas.

b. SO typically are an integral part of theater campaigns. While SO can be conducted unilaterally in support of specific theater or national objectives, the majority of SO are designed and conducted to enhance the likelihood of success of the overall theater campaign. SO must complement—not compete with nor be a substitute for—conventional operations.

c. The successful conduct of **SO rely on individuals and small units proficient** in specialized skills trained to be applied with adaptability, improvisation, and innovation. While organized for independent operations, SOF effectiveness can often be enhanced when SOF are supported by non-SOF organizations. SO normally require precise tactical-level planning, detailed intelligence, and knowledge of the culture(s) and language(s) of the areas in which the missions are to be conducted. **Rigorous training and mission rehearsals** are integral to the conduct of most SO. SO conducted by small-size SOF units with unique capabilities and self-sufficiency (for short periods of time) provide the United States with additional options for feasible and appropriate military responses. These responses may result in lower degrees of political liability or risk of escalation than are normally associated with employment of larger and more visible CF.

d. **SO can be conducted directly** against an adversary in a single engagement, such as direct action (DA) against critical communication nodes, **or indirectly,** by organizing, training, and supporting insurgent forces through unconventional warfare (UW) against a hostile government or occupying force, or supporting an HN force in support of a friendly government through foreign internal defense (FID) and/or security force assistance (SFA). Other indirect methods include military information support operations (MISO) to influence the adversary military or local civilian populace and civil affairs operations (CAO) to provide essential support to a JFC responsible for civil-military operations (CMO). The results of SO are consistently disproportionate to the size of the units involved.

e. Deployed SOF for some mission profiles will require key CF enablers to maximize their operational effectiveness. These enablers are categorized by battlefield operating systems: maneuver; mobility, countermobility, and survivability; fire support; air defense; intelligence; combat service support; and C2. These CF enablers that enhance SOF capabilities vary by the SOF mission requirements and the SOF disposition in relation to CF (varying in scope from collocation with CF to complete isolation).

3. Special Operations Across the Range of Military Operations

a. JP 3-0, *Joint Operations,* states the nature of joint operations requires a JFC to organize and employ joint forces to achieve strategic and operational objectives. Each joint operation (and special operation) has a unique political and strategic context, so the balance and nature of military activities applied will vary according to the unique aspects of the mission and operational environment.

b. Military operations, to include SO, vary in scope, purpose, and combat intensity. A fundamental construct that provides context to the intensity of conflict that may occur during joint military activities is the **range of military operations:** from recurring military engagement, security cooperation, and deterrence activities (typically no conflict to low-intensity conflict), to crisis response and limited contingency operations (low to high), and if necessary, to major operations and campaigns (high intensity) as depicted in Figure I-1.

(1) Use of SOF and SO, concurrent with CF capabilities in **military engagement, security cooperation, and deterrence** activities help shape the operational environment and keep the day-to-day tensions between nations or groups below the threshold of armed conflict, which serves to maintain US global influence.

(2) SOF, whether employed independently or complementing CF, participate in many of the missions associated with **crisis response and limited contingencies,** such as CMO, FID, and SFA.

(3) Individual **major operations and campaigns** often contribute to a larger, long-term effort (e.g., Operation ENDURING FREEDOM). For those large scale efforts, SOF and SO are typically part of the shaping of the operational environment, and may conduct significant activities (e.g., CT and COIN) as part of the campaign or operational effort. The nature of the security environment may require US joint forces, including SOF, to engage in several types of operations simultaneously across the range of military operations. For these missions, commanders synchronize offensive, defensive, and stability operations and activities as necessary to achieve objectives.

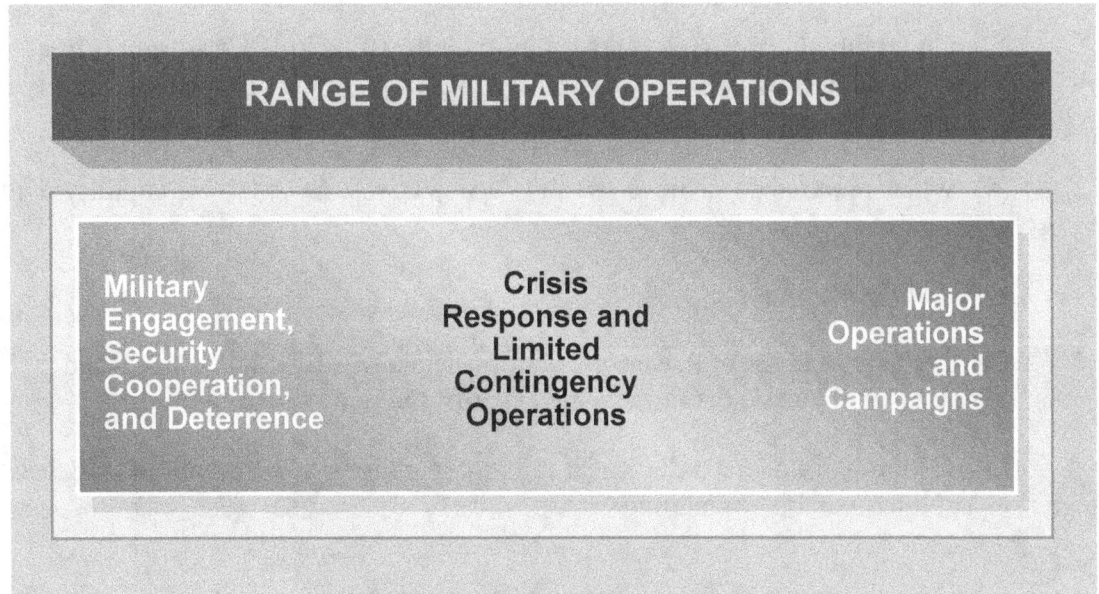

RANGE OF MILITARY OPERATIONS

| Military Engagement, Security Cooperation, and Deterrence | Crisis Response and Limited Contingency Operations | Major Operations and Campaigns |

Figure I-1. Range of Military Operations

c. The commander for any particular operation determines the emphasis to be placed on each type of mission or activity. Although specific types of operations are under the various joint military categories in the range of military operations, each type is not doctrinally fixed and could shift within that range. For example, a COIN operation could escalate from a security cooperation activity into a major operation or campaign.

d. SO can be conducted across the range of military operations at all levels of war and throughout all phases of a campaign or operation. While SO can be applied tactically, commanders and planners should focus SO on strategic and operational objectives and end states to maximize efficiency. Some SO are especially suitable for military engagement without conflict. SO provide options which in appropriate circumstances can prove to be the most viable means of achieving certain objectives. GCCs may leverage the theater special operations command (TSOC) to ensure full integration of SOF capabilities when developing theater plans. SO are most effective during crisis when SOF has had enough time (months to years) to conduct pre-crisis activities, build relationships, and build HN/PN SOF capacity as part of shaping operations (Phase 0) of theater campaign and contingency plans. Longer term preparations for SO provide options for decision makers in times of crisis that would otherwise not be available. Also, pre-crisis SO preparations may provide situational awareness that permits identification of a potential crisis prior to requiring a US military response, thus allowing a whole-of-government solution be applied to de-escalate the situation by dissuading, deterring, or disrupting the parties involved or through mediation.

(1) **The President designates national objectives** and sanctions the military means to achieve them. In pursuit of those objectives, some SO may be conducted under the direct supervision of the President or Secretary of Defense (SecDef).

(2) **Theater objectives are established by each GCC,** based on national strategic guidance, and are an integral part of a theater campaign plan. The GCC should consider integration of SO into the full range of military operations that supports the theater campaign plan and other theater plans.

(3) **Operational objectives established by subordinate JFCs support theater objectives and lead directly to theater success.** SO provide the JFC with a selective, flexible deterrent option or crisis response capability to achieve operational objectives.

(4) When required to achieve the JFC's objectives, SO may be conducted in support of CF and vice versa.

e. CF and SOF Integration:

(1) Exchange and use of liaison and control elements are critical when CF and SOF conduct operations in the same operational area against the same threat.

(2) A thorough understanding of a unit's capabilities and limitations enhances integration and interoperability planning.

(3) During mission planning, options should consider how to integrate CF and SOF maneuver elements. Detailed planning and execution coordination is required throughout the process.

(4) Successful integration and interoperability of CF and SOF are dependent upon understanding each other's systems, capabilities, and limitations.

f. **Presentation of Special Operations Forces.** United States Special Operations Command (USSOCOM) deploys and sustains SOF to facilitate operations with CF, to promote synergy among all SOF elements, and to provide more efficient C2 structures. For military engagement, security cooperation, and deterrence operations, forward based and distributed C2 nodes under the operational control (OPCON) of the TSOC provide the necessary C2 for assigned and attached SOF. For crisis response, contingency, and major operations and campaigns, SOF may deploy a special operations joint task force (SOJTF) where all SOF report to one SO commander and the packaged force includes all enabling capabilities (organic to SO formations and those Service-provided CF capabilities) required to optimize the effectiveness of the SOJTF. A SOJTF is an operational level organization that may have one or more subordinate joint special operations task forces (JSOTFs).

For a detailed discussion of the range of military operations, including the relationship to the instruments of national power, levels of war, and the categories of joint military activities, see JP 1, Doctrine for the Armed Forces of the United States, *and JP 3-0,* Joint Operations.

Intentionally Blank

CHAPTER II
SPECIAL OPERATIONS FORCES AND THEIR CORE ACTIVITIES

> *"Special Operations Forces are contributing globally well beyond what their percentage of the total force numbers would indicate. Every day they are fighting our enemies, training and mentoring our partners, and bringing value to tens of thousands of villagers who are still deciding their allegiances."*
>
> **Admiral Eric T. Olson**
> **Commander, United States Special Operations Command**
> **Statement to the House Armed Services Committee**
> **2 April 2009**

1. Introduction

JP 1, *Doctrine for the Armed Forces of the United States,* characterizes traditional warfare (or regular warfare), as a confrontation between nation-states or coalitions/alliances of nation-states involving small to large scale, force-on-force military operations in which adversaries employ a variety of conventional military capabilities against each other in the air, land, maritime, and space physical domains and the information environment (which includes cyberspace). JP 1, *Doctrine for the Armed Forces of the United States,* and JP 3-0, *Joint Operations,* both address irregular warfare (IW) as the pervasive form of warfare of choice by many state adversaries and transnational violent extremists, because of the superiority of the United States in traditional warfare. From the United States perspective, IW encompasses a level of conflict that is less than traditional warfare and involves an adversary seeking to disrupt or negate the military capabilities and advantages of a more powerful, conventionally armed military force, often representing the regime of a nation. However, the strategic objectives of IW are no less significant than those of traditional warfare. Unlike the force-on-force orientation of traditional warfare, IW focuses on the strategic purpose of gaining and maintaining control or influence over, and the support of a relevant population through political, psychological, and economic methods. IW requires a different mindset and different capabilities than those focused on the conventional military defeat of an adversary. The SOF mindset and capabilities make them particularly well suited for all forms of IW. Further, SOF capabilities complement those of CF, whom the Department of Defense (DOD) also has tasked with gaining a core competency in IW. This chapter focuses on who SOF are, their unique characteristics, and the activities they conduct to help attain US strategic objectives.

2. Designated Special Operations Forces

SOF are those forces identified in Title 10, United States Code (USC), Section 167 or those units or forces that have since been designated as SOF by SecDef. Generally, SOF are under the combatant command (command authority) (COCOM) of the commander, United States Special Operations Command (CDRUSSOCOM), or the respective GCC to which they are assigned. SOF are those Active Component and Reserve Component (RC) forces of the Services specifically organized, trained, and equipped to conduct and support SO.

a. **US Army.** Special forces (SF), Ranger, Army SO aviation, SO MISO, and SO civil affairs (CA) units.

b. **US Navy.** SEAL, SEAL delivery vehicle, and special boat teams.

c. **US Air Force.** SO flying units (includes unmanned aircraft systems), special tactics elements (includes combat control, pararescue, SO weather, and select tactical air control party [TACP] units), and aviation FID units.

d. **US Marine Corps.** Marine SO battalions which can be task organized to conduct specific SO missions in support of USSOCOM or a supported GCC.

e. Certain CF receive enhanced training and/or equipment to support SO and have developed habitual relationships with SOF units to conduct these missions.

3. Characteristics of Special Operations Forces

a. **SOF are inherently joint.** SOF regularly conduct joint and combined training, both within the SOF community and with CF. When employed, SOF are presented with their C2 structure intact, which facilitates their integration into joint force plans, retains cohesion, and provides a control mechanism to address SO specific concerns and coordinate their activities with other components and supporting commands. Across the range of military operations, SOF can conduct the broad range of SO including a surgical, rapid, worldwide strike capability. Additionally, SOF routinely operate closely with OGAs, intergovernmental organizations (IGOs), nongovernmental organizations (NGOs), and other nations' forces. The complex and sometimes clandestine/low visibility nature of SO and the demanding environments in which such operations are conducted require carefully selected, highly trained and educated, and experienced warriors. SOF require unique training and education, and may also require the development, acquisition, and employment of weapons and equipment not standard for other Armed Forces of the United States.

b. **SOF are distinct from CF.** Commanders should be familiar with these characteristics as well as the SOF capabilities and limitations to better select missions and tasks compatible with their capabilities.

(1) Most SOF personnel undergo a careful selection process and mission-specific training beyond basic military skills to achieve entry-level SO skills. These programs make rapid replacement or regeneration of personnel or capabilities unlikely.

(2) SOF organizational structures tend to be populated by mature and seasoned personnel, many of whom maintain high levels of competency in more than one military specialty.

(3) Selected SOF are regionally, culturally, and linguistically oriented for employment; extensive language and cross-cultural training are a routine part of their development.

c. **SOF Capabilities.** SOF can be formed into versatile, self-contained teams that provide a JFC with a flexible force capable of operating in ambiguous and swiftly changing scenarios. They can:

(1) Be task-organized quickly and deployed rapidly to provide tailored responses to many different situations.

(2) Gain access to hostile or denied areas.

(3) Provide limited medical support for themselves and those they support.

(4) Communicate worldwide with organic equipment.

(5) Conduct operations in austere, harsh environments without extensive support.

(6) Survey and assess local situations and report these assessments rapidly.

(7) Work closely with regional military and civilian authorities and populations.

(8) Organize people into working teams to help solve local problems.

(9) Deploy with a generally lower profile and less intrusive presence than CF.

(10) Provide unconventional options for addressing ambiguous situations.

d. **SOF Limitations**

(1) SOF cannot be quickly replaced or reconstituted nor can their capabilities be rapidly expanded. Improper employment of SOF (e.g., in purely conventional roles or on inappropriate or inordinately high-risk missions) runs the risk of rapidly depleting these resources.

(2) **SOF are not a substitute for CF.** In most cases SOF are neither trained, organized, nor equipped to conduct sustained conventional combat operations and, therefore, should not be substituted for CF that are able to effectively execute that mission.

(3) **Most SO missions require non-SOF support.** SOF are typically provided to GCCs and are not structured with robust means of logistic and sustainment capabilities. SOF must rely on the supported GCC's Service component commands for most support except for those SOF-unique assets that are required to be supplied by USSOCOM.

e. **SOF Mission Criteria.** The employment of SOF is facilitated by five basic criteria that provide guidelines for both SOF and CF commanders and planners when considering the employment of SOF (see Figure II-1.)

FIVE SPECIAL OPERATIONS FORCES MISSION CRITERIA

1. **Must be an appropriate special operations forces (SOF) mission or activity.**

2. **Mission or tasks should support the joint force commander's campaign or operation plan, or special activities.**

3. **Missions or tasks must be operationally feasible, approved, and fully coordinated.**

4. **Required resources must be available to execute and support the SOF mission.**

5. **The expected outcome of the mission must justify the risks.**

Figure II-1. Five Special Operations Forces Mission Criteria

(1) **It must be an appropriate mission or activity for SOF. SOF should normally be employed against targets with strategic or operational relevance.** SOF should be used to create effects that require SOF's unique skills and capabilities. If the mission or task does not require those skills and capabilities, SOF should not be employed.

(2) **The mission or activities should support the JFC's campaign or operation plan, or special activities.** If not, shortfall in SOF capabilities should be pointed out and appropriate SOF missions recommended.

(3) **Mission or tasks must be operationally feasible, approved, and fully coordinated.** SOF are not structured for attrition or force-on-force warfare and should not be assigned missions nor employed beyond their capabilities. For example, during planning and execution JFCs and SOF commanders and their staffs must consider the vulnerability of SOF units to larger, more heavily armed or mobile forces, particularly in a hostile environment. They should also synchronize their operations with those of other components within the operational area and coordinate the timing and location of support requirements with the appropriate commanders.

---

(4) **Required resources must be available to execute and support the SOF mission.** Some SOF missions require support from other forces for success, especially for long-term operations, and those operations supporting HNs with limited supporting assets. Such support involves aiding, protecting, complementing, and sustaining the employed SOF, and can include airlift, intelligence, communications, information operations (IO), medical, logistics, space, weather, chemical, biological, radiological, and nuclear (CBRN) defense, and other types of support. Although a target may be vulnerable to SOF, mission support deficiencies may affect the likelihood for success or may entirely invalidate the feasibility of employing SOF.

(5) **The expected outcome of the mission must justify the risks.** SOF are high-value assets and limited in numbers and resources. Commanders should ensure that the benefits of successful missions are measurable and in balance with the risks in the mission assessment. Risk management analysis should consider not only the potential loss of SOF units and equipment, but also the risk of adverse effects on US diplomatic and domestic political interests if the mission fails. While the use of SOF may present the potential for a proportionally greater influence on the JFC's campaign or operation, there are some operations that SOF can execute that will make only a marginal contribution while presenting a high risk of personnel and material loss. When contemplating SO, commanders must balance potential SOF losses against the potential operational gain.

4. **Special Operations Core Activities**

SOF are specifically organized, trained, and equipped to accomplish the 11 core activities listed in Figure II-2. **The core activities represent the collective capabilities of all joint SOF rather than those of any one Service or unit.** While CF also conduct many of these activities (e.g., FID, SFA, COIN, and CT), SOF conduct them using specialized tactics, techniques, and procedures, and to unique conditions and standards in a manner that complement CF capabilities. Use of SOF with CF creates an additional and unique capability to achieve objectives that may not be otherwise attainable. SOF can arrange and package their capabilities in combinations to provide DOD options applicable to a broad range of strategic and operational challenges. Additionally, SOF can perform other activities of a collateral nature such as counterdrug operations and noncombatant evacuation operations. SOF also conduct preparation of the environment as a type of shaping activity supporting core activities that may be conducted in the future.

a. **Direct Action.** DA entails short-duration strikes and other small-scale offensive actions conducted as SO in hostile, denied, or diplomatically sensitive environments, and which employ specialized military capabilities to seize, destroy, capture, exploit, recover, or damage designated targets. DA differs from conventional offensive actions in the level of diplomatic or political risk, the operational techniques employed, and the degree of discriminate and precise use of force to achieve specific objectives. In the conduct of these operations, SOF may employ raids, ambushes, or other direct assault tactics (including close-quarters combat); emplace mines and other munitions; conduct standoff attacks by fire from air, ground, or maritime platforms; provide terminal guidance for precision-guided munitions; conduct independent sabotage; conduct anti-ship operations, as well as ship boarding and seizure (e.g., maritime interception operations).

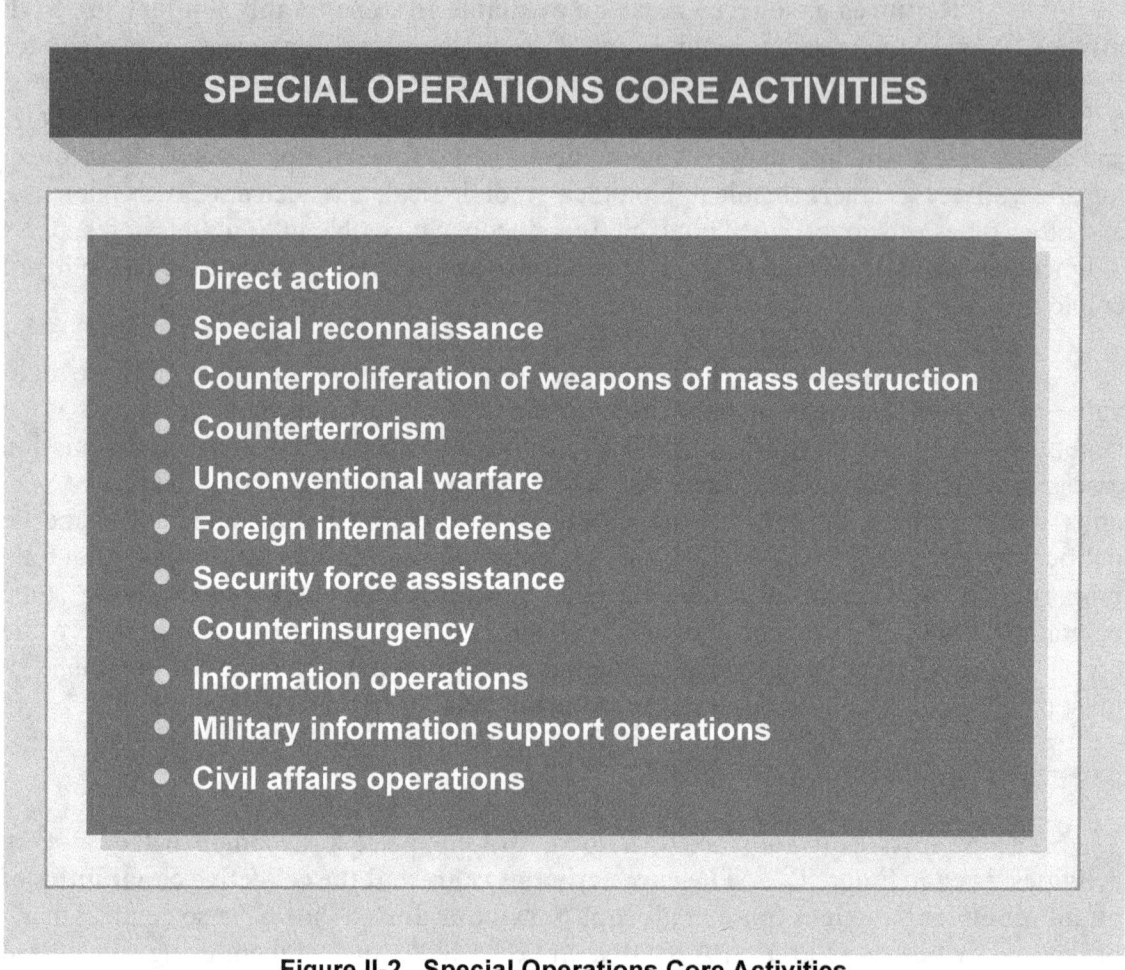

SPECIAL OPERATIONS CORE ACTIVITIES

- Direct action
- Special reconnaissance
- Counterproliferation of weapons of mass destruction
- Counterterrorism
- Unconventional warfare
- Foreign internal defense
- Security force assistance
- Counterinsurgency
- Information operations
- Military information support operations
- Civil affairs operations

Figure II-2. Special Operations Core Activities

(1) Normally limited in scope and duration, DA usually incorporates an immediate withdrawal from the planned objective area. These operations can provide specific, well-defined, and often time-sensitive results of critical significance at the operational and strategic levels of war.

(2) SOF may conduct DA independently or as part of larger conventional or unconventional operation or campaign. Although normally considered close combat DA also includes sniping and other standoff attacks by fire delivered or directed by SOF. Standoff attacks are preferred when the target can be damaged or destroyed without close combat. SOF employ close combat tactics and techniques when the mission requires precise or discriminate use of force or the recovery or capture of personnel or materiel.

(3) DA missions may also involve locating, recovering, and restoring to friendly control selected persons or materiel that are isolated and threatened in sensitive, denied, or contested areas. These missions usually result from situations that involve political sensitivity or military criticality of the personnel or materiel being recovered from remote or hostile environments. These situations may arise from a political change, combat action, chance happening, or mechanical mishap. DA usually differs from personnel recovery by

the former's use of dedicated ground combat elements, unconventional techniques, precise survivor-related intelligence, and indigenous assistance.

(4) DA, whether unilateral or combined, are short-duration, discrete actions. The SOF command executes DA to achieve the supported commander's objectives.

b. **Special Reconnaissance (SR).** SR entails reconnaissance and surveillance actions conducted as SO in hostile, denied, or diplomatically sensitive environments to collect or verify information of strategic or operational significance, employing military capabilities not normally found in CF. These actions provide an additive collection capability for commanders and supplement other conventional reconnaissance and surveillance actions. SR may include collecting information on activities of an actual or potential enemy or securing data on the meteorological, hydrographic, or geographic characteristics of a particular area. SR may also include assessment of chemical, biological, residual nuclear, radiological, or environmental hazards in a denied area. SR includes target acquisition, area assessment, and post-strike reconnaissance, and may be accomplished by air, land, or maritime assets.

(1) SR complements national and theater intelligence collection assets and systems by obtaining specific, well-defined, and time-sensitive information of strategic or operational significance. SR may also complement other collection methods constrained by weather, terrain-masking, or hostile countermeasures. Selected SOF conduct SR when authorized, to place "eyes on target" in hostile, denied, or diplomatically sensitive territory. SR typically provides essential information to develop a commander's situational awareness necessary for a command decision, follow-on mission, or critical assessment.

(2) Using SOF for SR enables the JFC to enhance situational awareness and facilitate staff planning and execution of joint operations, whether by CF, SOF, or integrated CF-SOF elements. However, CF-SOF integration does not mean that SOF will become dedicated reconnaissance assets for CF. Rather, the JFC typically tasks SOF through their JSOTF or TSOC to provide SR within a joint special operations area (JSOA), and/or the JFC may task SOF on a case-by-case basis to conduct SR within a CF's operational area.

(3) SOF may also employ advanced reconnaissance and surveillance sensors and collection methods that utilize indigenous assets.

c. **Counterproliferation (CP) of Weapons of Mass Destruction (WMD).** CP refers to actions taken to defeat the threat and/or use of WMD against the United States, our forces, allies, and partners. WMD are chemical, biological, radiological, or nuclear weapons capable of a high order of destruction or causing mass casualties and exclude the means of transporting or propelling the weapon where such means is a separable and divisible part from the weapon. The major objectives of combating WMD policy, which include nonproliferation, CP, and consequence mitigation activities, are to prevent the acquisition of WMD and delivery systems, to stop or roll back proliferation where it has occurred, to deter and defeat the use of WMD and their delivery systems, to adapt US military forces and planning to operate against the threats posed by WMD and their delivery systems, and to mitigate the effects of WMD use. The continued spread of WMD technology can foster regional unrest and provide terrorist organizations with new and potent weapons. SOF provide the following capabilities for this core activity:

(1) Expertise, materiel and teams to supported combatant command teams to locate, tag, and track WMD, as required.

(2) Capabilities to conduct DA in limited access areas, as required.

(3) Build partnership capacity for conducting CP activities.

(4) Conduct IO and MISO to dissuade adversary reliance on WMD.

(5) Other specialized capabilities to combat WMD.

For further information on CP of WMD, refer to JP 3-40, Combating Weapons of Mass Destruction.

d. **Counterterrorism.** Terrorism has evolved over several decades from a tactic of inducing fear in select populations to a transnational threat of strategic proportions, particularly against the United States, Western societies, and emerging democracies perpetuated primarily by groups of violent extremists. Today, whether the extremists are local insurgents or members of an international terrorist network, they are generally viewed as terrorists if they use terrorist tactics. Furthermore, the threat to US interests posed by violent extremists will increase as the continued proliferation of WMD presents an opportunity for terrorists to acquire and use them. CT is a form of IW.

(1) CT is defined as actions taken directly against terrorist networks and indirectly to influence and render global and regional environments inhospitable to terrorist networks. In addition to being a SOF core activity, CT is part of the DOD's broader construct of combating terrorism (CbT), which is actions, including antiterrorism and CT, taken to oppose terrorism throughout the entire threat continuum.

(2) The United States Government (USG) policy on CbT is to defeat violent extremism and create a global environment that is inhospitable to violent extremists. The broad USG strategy is to continue to lead an international effort to deny violent extremist networks the resources and functions they need to operate and survive. The DOD strategy for CbT implements the following objectives from the *National Strategy for Combating Terrorism*, objectives that are derived from the *National Security Strategy (NSS)*:

(a) Thwart or defeat terrorist attacks against the US, our PNs, and our interests.

(b) Attack and disrupt terrorist networks abroad so as to cause adversaries to be incapable or unwilling to attack the US homeland, allies, or interests.

(c) Deny terrorist networks WMD.

(d) Establish conditions that allow PNs to govern their territory effectively and defeat terrorists.

(e) Deny a hospitable environment to violent extremists.

(3) CDRUSSOCOM is responsible for synchronizing planning for global operations against terrorist networks, in coordination with other combatant commands, the Services and, as directed, appropriate USG agencies.

(4) Success in the global CT effort requires interorganizational coordination to maximize the effectiveness of all the instruments of national power of the United States and PNs. USSOCOM, as the integrating command for global CT planning efforts, supports a global combating terrorism network (GCTN)—a growing network of relationships and liaison partnerships, a supporting technical infrastructure, and the use of information sharing policies. Along with interagency partners, this network draws upon an increasing number of countries, regional organizations, IGOs, NGOs, and the private sector to achieve unified action.

(5) The DOD global campaign plan for the war on terrorism requires integration of both the direct and indirect approaches. The ability to manage both approaches and harness their synergistic effects is vital to the success of both near- and long-term CT objectives, whether within the scope of a theater operation/campaign of a GCC, or the global campaign.

(a) **Direct Approach.** The direct approach consists of actions taken against terrorists and terrorist organizations to disrupt or defeat a specific threat through neutralization or destruction of the network (including individuals, resources, and support structures) and to prevent the reemergence of a threat. This approach may include the use of SOF core activities such as CT, SR, DA, MISO, IO, CAO, and CP.

(b) **Indirect Approach.** The indirect approach consists of the means by which the GCTN can influence the operational environments within which CT operations/campaigns are conducted. This approach usually includes actions taken to enable GCTN partners to conduct operations against terrorists and their organizations as well as actions taken to shape and stabilize their operational environments as a means to erode the capabilities of terrorist organizations and degrade their ability to acquire support and sanctuary. The indirect approach includes use of the SOF core activities such as FID, SFA, IO, MISO, and CAO. These activities combined with stability operations, counterintelligence, CMO, and strategic communication produce synergies to enable partners to combat terrorist organization, deter tacit and active support for terrorism, and erode support for terrorist ideologies.

For further information on CT, refer to JP 3-26, Counterterrorism.

e. **Unconventional Warfare.** UW are those activities conducted to enable a resistance movement or insurgency to coerce, disrupt, or overthrow a government or occupying power by operating through or with an underground, auxiliary, and guerrilla force in a denied area. The United States may engage in UW across the spectrum of armed conflict from major campaigns to limited contingency operations. The US has conducted UW in support of insurgent movements attempting to overthrow an adversarial regime as well as in support of resistance movements to defeat occupying powers (e.g., the Nicaraguan Contras and the

Afghan Mujahedeen). UW was also successfully used against the Taliban in the initial stages of Operation ENDURING FREEDOM in Afghanistan. UW can be an effective way of putting indirect and direct pressure on a hostile government or occupying power.

(1) Military leaders must carefully consider the costs and benefits prior to making a recommendation to engage in UW. Properly coordinated and executed UW may help set conditions for international crisis resolution on terms favorable to the United States or allies without the need for an overt US CF commitment.

(2) The conduct of UW can have a strategic military-politico utility that can alter the balance of power between sovereign states, and there is potentially significant political risk both at home and abroad. The paramilitary aspect of UW may place DOD in a supporting role to interorganizational partners. The necessity to operate with a varying mix of clandestine/covert means and ways places a premium on operations security (OPSEC) and all-source intelligence. In UW, as in all conflict scenarios, US military forces must closely coordinate their activities with interorganizational partners to enable and safeguard sensitive operations.

(3) A JFC typically tasks SOF to conduct the military aspect of UW. It will usually require support relationships with some interagency partners and some Service components. A JFC and staff must be able to conduct/support UW operations simultaneously during both traditional warfare and/or IW.

(4) While each UW mission is unique, US-sponsored UW generally includes seven phases: preparation, initial contact, infiltration, organization, build-up, employment, and transition. These phases may occur concurrently in some situations or may not be required in others. For example, a large established resistance movement may only require initial contact and build up of logistical support to begin UW activities, thereby bypassing the other earlier phases of preparation, infiltration, and organization. The phases also may occur out of sequence, with each receiving varying degrees of emphasis, such as when members of an indigenous irregular force are moved to another country to be trained, organized, and equipped before being infiltrated back into the designated operational area, either with or without US SOF.

(5) Senior civilian leaders and JFCs should understand that UW operations require time to mature and reach maximum effectiveness, especially when all of the insurgent or resistance underground networks have to be established.

f. **Foreign Internal Defense.** From the US perspective, FID refers to the US activities that support a HN's internal defense and development (IDAD) strategy designed to protect against subversion, lawlessness, insurgency, terrorism, and other threats to their security, stability, and legitimacy. As shown in Figure II-3, characteristics of FID involve the instruments of national power (diplomatic, informational, military, and economic) through which elements of that power (e.g., financial, intelligence, and law enforcement) can be applied to support a HN's IDAD program. The US FID effort is tailored to the needs of the individual nation or region.

(1) SOF units typically contribute to a FID effort under the OPCON of a TSOC commander, conducting FID operations other than combat, and may require the participating SOF chain of command to have a direct coordination relationship with the chief of mission (COM) or another designee at the appropriate US embassy. In smaller FID operations, SOF units may compose the majority, if not the entire US force. The opposite may be true in a large-scale FID operation, where limits on total troop numbers may result in a smaller number of SOF personnel than CF. In some cases, long-term FID operations may be initiated by SOF, then handed over to CF.

(2) SOF may conduct FID operations unilaterally in the absence of any other military effort, or in support of other ongoing military (i.e., CF) or civilian assistance efforts.

CHARACTERISTICS OF FOREIGN INTERNAL DEFENSE

- Involves all instruments of national power.
- Can occur across the range of military operations.
- Is conducted by both conventional forces and special operations forces.
- Supports and influences a host nation's internal defense and development program.
- Includes training, materiel, technical and organizational assistance, advice, infrastructure development, and tactical operations.
- Generally, the preferred methods of support are through assistance and development programs.

Figure II-3. Characteristics of Foreign Internal Defense

FID also supports stability operations designed to promote and protect US national interests by influencing adversarial, political, and information operational variables in a region or country through a combination of peacetime developmental, cooperative activities, and coercive crisis response actions when necessary.

(3) All SOF Service components have capabilities that can contribute to a FID effort. The primary roles of SOF in FID are to assess, train, advise, and assist HN military and paramilitary forces with activities that require the unique capabilities of SOF. As previously mentioned, SOF may also conduct specialized missions in support of combat operations. The goal is to enable HN forces to maintain the internal stability, to counter subversion and violence in their country, and to address the causes of instability. Each of these key activities plays a role in the accomplishment of the HN IDAD strategy through HN military assistance, population security, and COIN.

(4) FID operations are planned at the national, regional, and especially with SOF units at the local level. FID should involve the integration of all instruments of national power down to the local level. FID operations fall under two major categories—those under the responsibility of DOD and those under the responsibility of the Department of State (DOS) and OGAs. FID has certain aspects that make planning for it complex. Basic imperatives to successfully integrate FID into strategies and plans include the planner having an understanding of US foreign policy; a focus to maintain or increase HN sovereignty and legitimacy; and an understanding of the long-term or strategic implications and sustainability of US assistance efforts. SOF support of FID programs should be tailored to operational, environment, and HN needs. Because FID is a national-level effort involving numerous USG agencies, unity of effort is important.

For further information on FID, refer to JP 3-22, Foreign Internal Defense.

g. **Security Force Assistance.** USG security sector reform (SSR) activities focus on the inextricably linked governmental sectors of security and justice. DOD's primary role in SSR is supporting the reform, restructuring, or reestablishment of the armed forces and the defense sector, which is accomplished through SFA. SFA specifically pertains to those DOD activities that contribute to unified action by the USG to support the development of the capacity and capability of foreign security forces (FSF) and their supporting institutions. FSF include but are not limited to military forces; police forces; border police, coast guard, and customs officials; paramilitary forces; interior and intelligence services; forces peculiar to specific nations, states, tribes, or ethnic groups; prison, correctional, and penal services; and the government ministries or departments responsible for the above services. The US military engages in activities to enhance the capabilities and capacities of a PN (or regional security organization) by providing training, equipment, advice, and assistance to those FSF organized under the equivalent of a national ministry of defense (or an equivalent regional military or paramilitary force), while other USG agencies focus on those FSF assigned to other ministries such as interior, justice, or intelligence services.

(1) USSOCOM is the designated joint proponent for SFA, with responsibility to lead the collaborative development, coordination, and integration of the SFA capability across DOD. This includes development of SFA joint doctrine; training and education for

individuals and units; joint capabilities; joint mission essential task lists; and identification of critical individual skills, training, and experience. Additionally, in collaboration with the Joint Staff and United States Joint Forces Command (USJFCOM), and in coordination with the Services and GCCs, USSOCOM is tasked with developing global joint sourcing solutions that recommend the most appropriate forces (CF and/or SOF) for a SFA mission.

(2) SFA includes activities of organizing, training, equipping, rebuilding, and advising various components of FSF. SOF/CF performing SFA conduct initial assessment of the FSF they will assist and then establish a shared way to continue assessing them throughout their development. The HN/PN determines the structure of its military forces, to include approving all organizational designs. These may include changing the numbers of forces, types of units, and internal organizational designs.

(3) Conducting successful SFA operations requires an advisor's mindset and dedication to working through or with FSF. The responsible CCDR tasking US forces to conduct SFA must emphasize that legitimacy is vital for both the US and its partners.

(4) FID and SFA are similar at the tactical level where advisory skills are applicable to both. At operational and strategic levels, both FID and SFA focus on preparing FSF to combat lawlessness, subversion, insurgency, terrorism, and other internal threats to their security; however, SFA also prepares FSF to defend against external threats and to perform as part of an international force. Although FID and SFA are both subsets of security cooperation, neither are considered subsets of the other.

For further information on FID and SFA, refer to JP 3-22, Foreign Internal Defense.

h. **Counterinsurgency.** COIN refers to the comprehensive civilian and military efforts taken to defeat insurgency and to address any core grievances. The combat skills, experience, cultural awareness, and language skills of SOF allow them to conduct a wide array of missions working through or with HN security forces or integrated with US CF, which make them particularly suitable for COIN operations or campaigns.

(1) **Operational Approaches.** There are three primary operational approaches to COIN: direct, indirect, and balanced. The direct approach focuses on protecting US and HN interests while attacking the insurgents. The indirect approach focuses on establishing conditions (a stable and more secure environment) for others to achieve success with the help of the US. The balanced approach is a combination of the direct and indirect methods. **Commanders adjust their approach as circumstances change, but the COIN approach should strive to move from direct to balanced, and ultimately to indirect.** However, the scale of effort for any approach will vary according to operational requirements and overall objectives for the COIN operations or campaign.

(a) **Direct.** A direct approach may be required where an HN government is losing ground in its struggle with an insurgency or there is no viable HN government. The first task in this situation is to establish security and control in as wide an area and extent as possible.

(b) **Indirect.** An indirect approach utilizes more development and diplomatic efforts than military efforts to address the insurgency. This approach is best suited to early intervention but requires that the HN be viable and viewed as legitimate.

(c) **Balanced.** The balanced approach is a more even blend of US diplomatic, developmental, and military efforts. Military efforts are secondary and subordinate to diplomatic and development activities when using this approach.

(2) **SOF Contributions to COIN.** The SOF contribution to COIN is critical through all approaches. Their role as warfighters in the direct approach provide the capabilities for urgent, necessary, and largely lethal activities, often with immediate impact—and to create time for the balanced and indirect approaches. SOF are well suited for the balanced and indirect approaches as combat trainers and advisors as well as warfighters. SOF assistance can increase the capability and capacity of HN specialized or irregular units, which helps mitigate manpower and leadership problems common among HN forces in COIN operations or campaigns. SOF also bring the unique capability to quickly adapt their skills with very little additional training to provide decision makers with a responsive tool to achieve US national objectives while avoiding the large footprint that would accompany CF. CA can provide key development assistance in contested areas. All SOF Service components have capabilities that can contribute to a COIN effort.

(3) **Relationship of Other Core Activities to COIN.** COIN is normally conducted as part of a larger FID program supporting the HN government. SOF can also perform a number of other core activities in support of COIN operations seeking to gain credibility with the relevant population. US applications of MISO and CAO can help reinforce the HN's legitimacy and capabilities and reduce insurgent influence over the population. SFA can range from standing up ministries to improving the organization of the smallest security unit and as such is integral to successful COIN operations. CT can be conducted when terrorism is used in an insurgency. COIN also involves SR and DA operations conducted against insurgents and their bases.

(4) **Defining the Operational Environment.** One of the key contributions of SOF during the preparatory phases of a COIN operation is to help define the operational environment and prepare for the entry of CF and supporting governmental agencies. This is accomplished through assessments, shaping, and intelligence activities, some derived from nontraditional sources. SOF assist in the development of cultural intelligence, measure perceptions and attitudes of the population, gain situational awareness through area reconnaissance, and can operate covertly/clandestinely in areas where CF cannot.

(5) **Center of Gravity.** The typical COIN strategic center of gravity is the indigenous population—thus the need to protect the population and gain and maintain popular support. When conducting operations, US forces adhere to the principle of measured and precise use of force—employing proportionality and discrimination. SOF, by their training, regional familiarity, cultural awareness, and understanding of social dynamics within relevant populations focus on establishing cooperative relationships with indigenous populations and with HN security forces to enhance the legitimacy of the government with the population in accordance with the HN IDAD plan.

For more information on COIN, refer to JP 3-24, Counterinsurgency Operations.

i. **Information Operations.** IO are the integrated employment, during military operations, of information-related capabilities in concert with other lines of operation to influence, disrupt, corrupt, or usurp the decision making of adversaries and potential adversaries while protecting our own. When properly coordinated, integrated, and synchronized as a part of the overall operation, IO affect the quality, content, and availability of information available to decision makers. IO also influence the perceptions and motivations of targeted key audiences with the goal of convincing them to act in a manner conducive to established objectives and desired end states. IO are conducted throughout all operational phases, across the range of military operations, and at every level of war.

(1) IO play a key role in the successful accomplishment of SO missions and promote other SOF core activities. For example, electronic warfare (EW) and computer network operations (CNO) disrupt adversary communications and networks while protecting our own fundamental conditions for successful SO missions. Similarly, OPSEC denies the adversary information needed to correctly assess SOF capabilities and intentions. MISO, a vital component of IO and a key SOF activity, can be employed to optimize the psychological impacts (positive or negative) of other SO activities (e.g., CT or COIN) on a variety of target audiences (TAs) and undermine an adversary's will to fight. Military deception (MILDEC) deliberately misleads adversary decision makers as to friendly military capabilities, intentions, and operations. When interwoven with EW and CNO, MILDEC can drive an adversary to take specific actions (or not take action), ultimately contributing to the efficacy of SOF activities (e.g., DA).

(2) In a similar fashion, other SOF activities complement IO and provide assistance toward the accomplishment of strategic and operational IO-related objectives. For example, SR and DA may identify, observe, target, disrupt, capture, or destroy specific capabilities tied to an adversary's C2 (i.e., decision making) processes. Further, successful FID, UW, COIN, and SFA can have a significant psychological impact on an adversary's morale or deliver a detrimental blow to the adversary's ability to recruit and finance operations. SOF may also play a key role in MILDEC by replicating the tactical impact of a much larger force presence.

(3) SOF leaders and staffs must integrate IO throughout all phases of an operation to protect critical capabilities and information, reduce overall risk to the mission and forces, and increase the prospect of mission success. The role of the IO planner is to coordinate, integrate, deconflict, and synchronize IO, and the supporting and related capabilities, whether CF- or SOF-provided, in accordance with the commander's objectives and selected courses of action (COAs). Likewise, the IO cell within the SOF headquarters (HQ) performs the critical function of optimizing the combined effects of SO activities and IO within the information environment; as related to stated SOF objectives, as well as larger operational and strategic end states.

(4) USSOCOM plays a broader, integrating role for IO in support of SOF across the combatant commands. As directed by the Unified Command Plan, USSOCOM integrates and coordinates DOD MISO capabilities to enhance interoperability, and supports

United States Strategic Command (USSTRATCOM) with its IO responsibilities and other CCDRs with MISO planning and execution. Additionally, USSOCOM supports the strategic and operational planning, oversight, and execution of IO and provides IO functional expertise and leadership by assisting in the development of policy, doctrine, future force plans, as well as conducting oversight/coordination of IO requirements for SOF. This includes development, education, joint IO training, experimentation, and advanced technology initiatives.

For further information on IO, refer to JP 3-13, Information Operations.

j. **Military Information Support Operations.** MISO are planned operations to convey selected information and indicators to foreign audiences to influence their emotions, motives, objective reasoning, and ultimately the behavior of foreign governments, organizations, groups, and individuals. The purpose of MISO is to induce or reinforce foreign attitudes and behavior favorable to the originator's objectives.

(1) MISO should be integrated during all phases of operations/campaigns, with both SOF and CF. Effective MISO require the commander's emphasis and active involvement. SO MISO forces and staff planners support the commander by integrating MISO throughout the operation. MISO are executed within carefully reviewed and approved programs and under mission-tailored approval guidelines that flow from national-level authorities.

(2) MISO planners follow a deliberate but responsive process that aligns commander's objectives with a thorough analysis of the environment; select relevant TAs; develop focused, culturally and environmentally tuned messages and actions; employ sophisticated media delivery means and produce observable, measurable behavioral response. However, MISO is most successful when fully synchronized and integrated with complementary actions by the larger joint force and other USG capabilities. The US military message must be congruent with US military actions if TAs are to be persuaded by MISO to modify short-term attitudes and perceptions and long-term behavior.

(3) Effective MISO are continuously planned and conducted across the range of military operations and throughout all phases of operations. In peacetime and limited crises response operations, MISO forces and activities are usually planned and coordinated through the TSOC. In permissive or uncertain environments not involving combat operations, MISO activities are planned and integrated with other operations and with other USG efforts to further national defense strategies through the GCC's theater campaign plan. In major contingencies, the JFC may establish a separate JSOTF known as the joint military information support operations task force (JMISOTF) to conduct MISO.

(4) MISO may be employed within the US under limited circumstances. During natural disasters or national security crises, MISO forces may deploy civil authority information support elements (CAISEs) supporting the designated lead federal agency to support civil authorities. SOF and CF MISO specialists, as part of CAISEs, may provide MISO for civil support (i.e., defense support of civil authorities) following natural disasters or other major crises.

(a) When authorized for employment in this manner, MISO forces inform rather than influence by utilizing their media development, production, and dissemination capabilities to deliver administrative and command information to populations in the operational area. Messages typically include information such as the location of relief sites, how to obtain essential services, disease prevention tips, current civil authority instructions, and similar messages. MISO dissemination assets such as radio broadcast systems, print production, and loudspeaker teams also can augment civilian commercial broadcast capabilities.

(b) All CAISE efforts are coordinated with ongoing military and lead federal agency public affairs (PA) activities as required.

(5) MISO play a key role in SO and in relation to each of the other SOF core activities; particularly in irregular conflicts that focus on ideological and social-political dimensions such as FID, COIN, CT, and UW. For example, MISO military information support teams may deploy to support approved COIN operations, demining, or foreign humanitarian assistance programs under either JFC or US diplomatic control. MISO staff planners and supporting MISO units provide the detailed planning and execution to reduce operational risk, enlist the aid of key populations, and optimize the impact of SO on the achievement of command objectives and USG policy.

(6) USSOCOM retains the preponderance of active duty MISO forces under United States Army Special Operations Command. USSOCOM also gains Air RC MISO forces through Air Force Special Operations Command when those Air National Guard assets are mobilized. To provide a strategic level MISO capability, USSOCOM established the Joint Military Information Support Command (JMISC), a joint subordinate command to serve as a key contributor in DOD's ongoing efforts to erode adversary power, will, and influence. JMISC plans, coordinates, integrates, and manages the execution of transregional information programs to achieve operational, strategic, and national goals and objectives. USSOCOM is the designated DOD proponent for MISO with the responsibility of coordinating the collaborative development and integration of DOD MISO.

For further information on MISO, refer to JP 3-13.2, Military Information Support Operations.

k. **Civil Affairs Operations.** CAO are operations conducted by CA forces that enhance the relationship between military forces and civil authorities in localities where military forces are present. This requires coordination with OGAs, IGOs, NGOs, indigenous populations and institutions, and the private sector. It involves application of CA functional specialty skills that are normally the responsibility of civil government to enhance planned CMO. All CMO must be synchronized and support the commander's intent and operational concept. All CA core tasks support the JFC's CMO objectives.

(1) CAO performed in support of SO are characterized by actions conducted by small CA teams or elements generally without the support of larger military formations, in isolated, austere, and in many cases politically-sensitive environments. Such CAO are unique and require flexibility and ingenuity from CA teams. Successful employment

requires planning and support from the CA staff at the supported TSOC. Additionally, these operations require a greater level of planning and coordination with multiple civilian and military partners for decentralized execution.

(2) CA personnel, leaders, and forces receive advanced skills training specific to CAO. CA teams are trained to identify critical (civil) vulnerabilities, conduct civil reconnaissance, engage HN and interagency counterparts, create country or region specific supporting plans, develop a series of activities to ensure unity of effort to achieve JFC and TSOC objectives, oversee projects, and eventually close activities and actions with assessments and targeting refinement. CA team members should be organized, trained, and prepared to serve as the senior SOF representative in countries with a limited SOF footprint. Figure II-4 depicts the relationship of CAO to overall unified action.

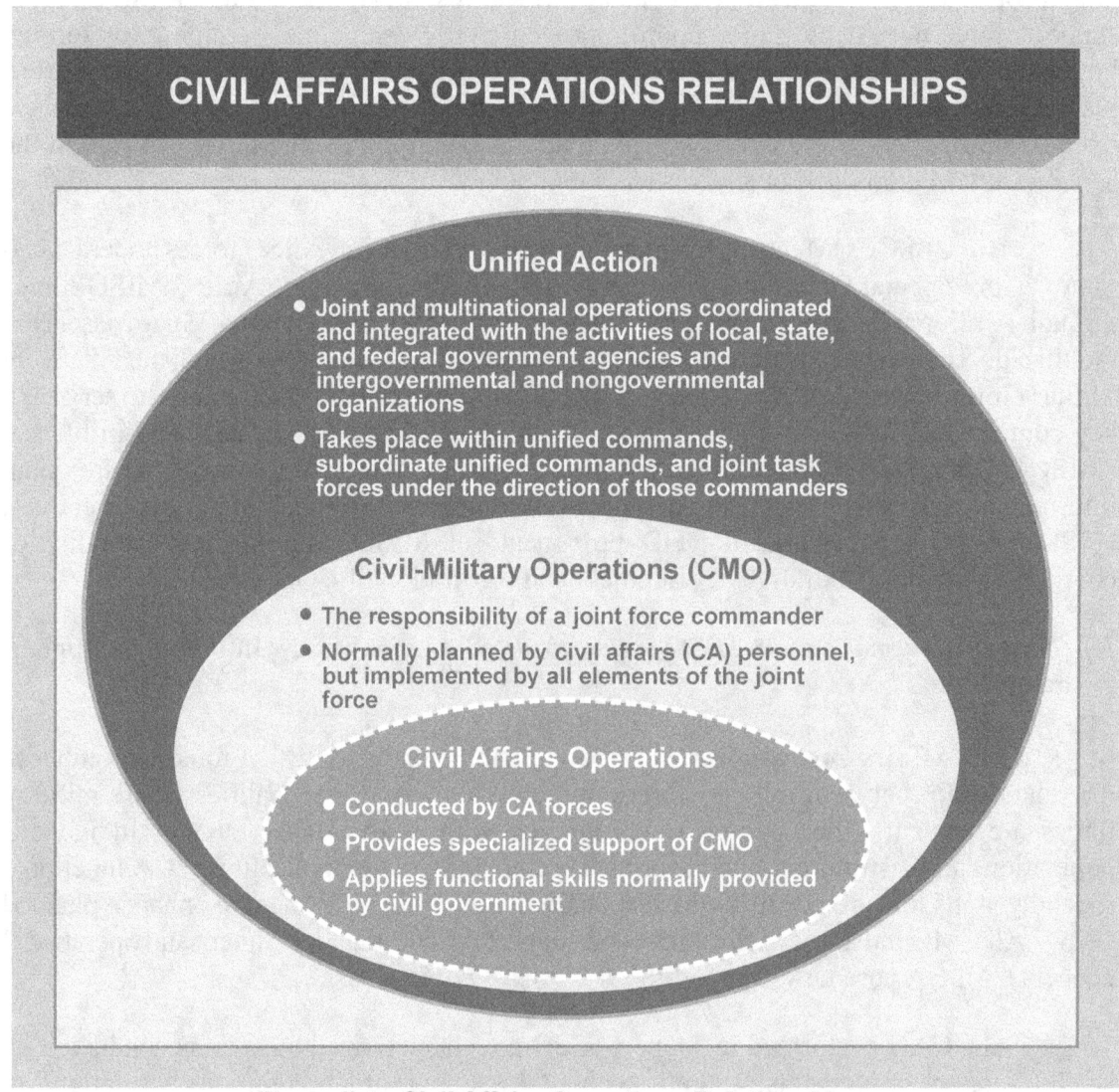

Figure II-4. Civil Affairs Operations Relationships

(3) CAO consist of those actions taken to coordinate with HN military and civilian agencies, OGAs, NGOs, or IGOs, in order to support US policy or the military commander's assigned mission. CA core tasks include:

    (a) Populace and resources control,

    (b) Foreign humanitarian assistance,

    (c) Nation assistance,

    (d) Support to civil administrations, and

    (e) Civil information management.

(4) CAO are conducted by CA forces organized, trained, and equipped to provide specialized support to commanders conducting CMO. Commanders having responsibility for an operational area typically will also have responsibility for the civilian populace therein. Commanders conduct CMO to establish, maintain, influence, or exploit relations between military forces and civilian authorities (governmental and nongovernmental) and the civilian populace in a permissive or hostile operational environment to facilitate military operations and to consolidate operational objectives. CA forces may assist in performance of activities and functions by military forces that are normally the responsibility of local government. CMO may be conducted before or during military operations and especially during stability operations.

For further information on CAO, refer to JP 3-57, Civil-Military Operations.

Intentionally Blank

CHAPTER III
COMMAND AND CONTROL OF SPECIAL OPERATIONS FORCES

"If officers desire to have control over their commands, they must remain habitually with them, industriously attend to their instruction and comfort, and in battle lead them well."

General Thomas Jonathan "Stonewall" Jackson
Letter of Instruction to Commanding Officers
Winchester, Virginia, 1861

1. Introduction

a. Command is the most important function undertaken by a JFC as it is the exercise of authority and direction by a properly designated commander over assigned and attached forces. C2 is the means by which a JFC synchronizes and/or integrates joint force activities to achieve unity of command, ties together all the operational functions and activities, and applies to all levels of war and echelons of command across the range of military operations. Effective C2 is a force multiplier that allows commanders to employ their forces toward a common effort. C2 should have a feedback process, or reciprocal influence, that allows commanders to best adapt to rapidly changing circumstances.

b. **SOF may be assigned to either CDRUSSOCOM or a GCC.** C2 of SOF normally should be executed within a SOF chain of command. The identification of a C2 organizational structure for SOF should depend upon specific objectives, security requirements, and the operational environment. Command relationships should be fashioned to provide the necessary guidance given an uncertain, noncontiguous, and asymmetric operational environment without unnecessarily restricting the initiative and flexibility of subordinate commanders. In all cases, commanders exercising command authority over SOF should:

(1) Provide for a clear and unambiguous chain of command.

(2) Avoid frequent transfer of SOF between commanders.

(3) Provide for sufficient staff experience and expertise to plan, conduct, and support the operations.

(4) Integrate SOF early in the planning process.

(5) Match unit capabilities with mission requirements.

c. **SOF are most effective when SO are fully integrated into the overall plan.** The ability of SOF to operate unilaterally, independently as part of the overall plan, or in support of a conventional commander requires a robust C2 structure for integration and coordination of the SOF effort. Successful SO require centralized, responsive, and unambiguous C2 through an appropriate SOF C2 element. The limited window of opportunity and sensitive nature of many SOF missions requires a C2 structure that is, above all, responsive to the needs of the operational unit and provides the most flexibility and agility in the application of SOF. SOF C2 may be tailored for a specific mission or operation.

d. **Liaison** among all components of the joint force and SOF, however they are organized, is vital for effective SOF employment, as well as coordination, deconfliction, synchronization, and the prevention of fratricide.

2. Assignment of Special Operations Forces

a. **SOF in the United States.** Unless otherwise directed by SecDef, all SOF based in the continental United States are assigned to USSOCOM and under the COCOM of CDRUSSOCOM. USSOCOM is a unified command (Title 10, USC, Section 167) that has the responsibilities of a functional combatant command and responsibilities similar to a Military Department in areas unique to SO. When directed as a supported commander by the President or SecDef, CDRUSSOCOM plans and conducts certain SO missions worldwide, in coordination with the applicable GCCs.

(1) In its role as a functional combatant command and when directed, USSOCOM provides US-based SOF on a temporary basis to other GCCs for operational employment. When transferred, the forces are **attached** to the gaining combatant command with the GCC normally exercising OPCON over them.

(2) When directed by the President or SecDef, CDRUSSOCOM can establish and employ task forces as a supported commander.

b. **SOF in Theater**

(1) The Armed Forces are predominantly CF and tend to operate as an integrated joint team across the range of military operations using a C2 structure centered on the JFC's mission and concept of operations, available forces and staff capabilities, location, and facilities. The JFC is typically a CF commander, and C2 is guided by principles of simplicity, span of control, unit integrity, and interoperability. This classic C2 framework is based on the *preponderance of forces* and the capability to control them.

(2) SOF assigned to a GCC are under the COCOM of the respective GCC. A GCC normally exercises OPCON of all assigned and attached SOF through the commander, theater special operations command (CDRTSOC) or a subordinate JFC. The CDRTSOC also may be designated as the joint force special operations component commander (JFSOCC) by the GCC (see Figure III-1). TSOCs and their subordinate SOF organizations and C2 coordination and liaison elements ensure that SO are responsive to the needs of the supported JFC, whether the JFC is a GCC or a CJTF.

(3) When a GCC establishes and employs multiple joint task forces (JTFs) and independent task forces, the TSOC commander may establish and employ multiple JSOTFs to manage SOF assets and accommodate JTF/task force SO requirements. Accordingly, the GCC, as the common superior commander, normally will establish supporting or tactical control (TACON) command relationships between JSOTF commanders and JTF/task force commanders.

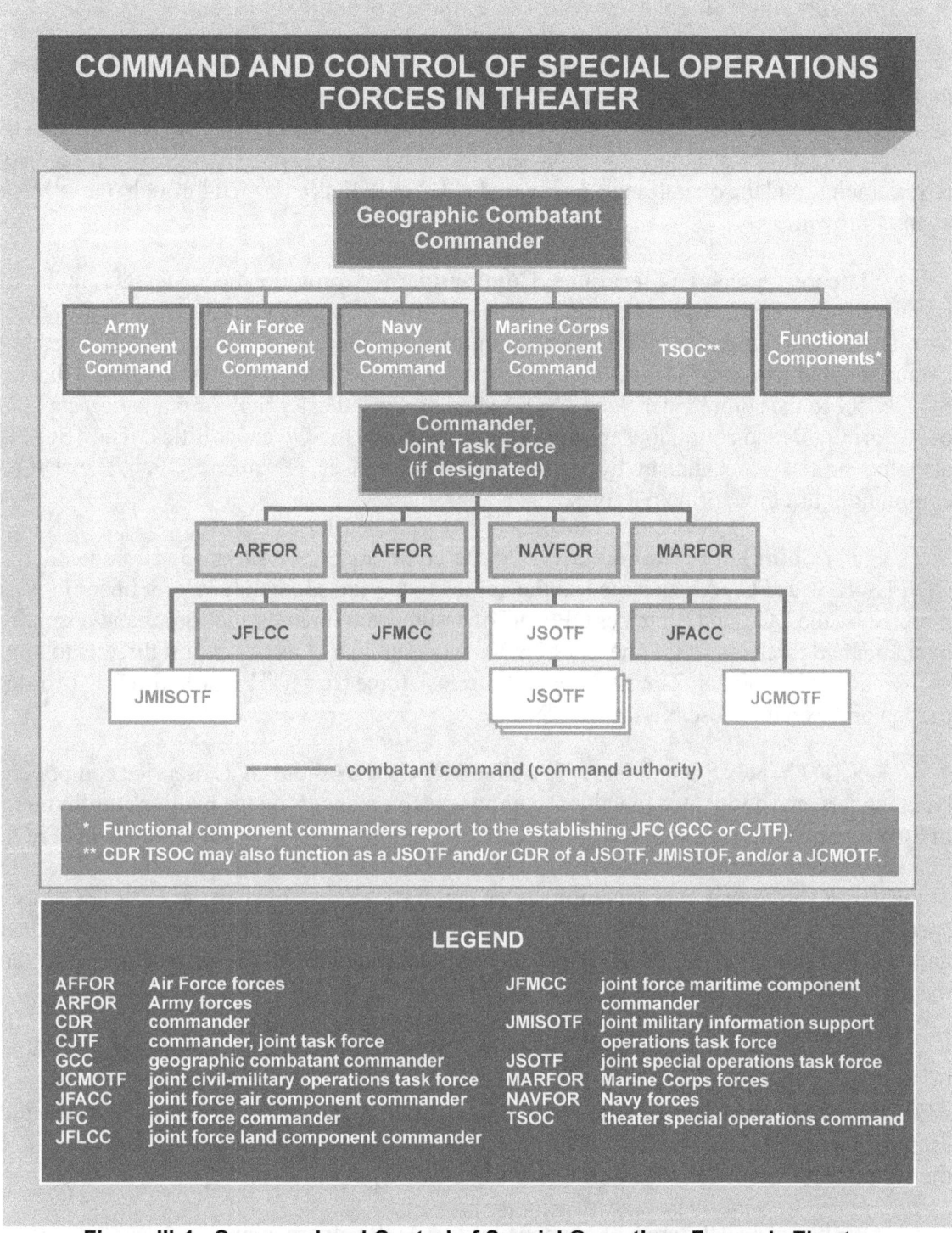

Figure III-1. Command and Control of Special Operations Forces in Theater

c. **SOF under control of a non-US command.** When directed by the President or SecDef through the Chairman of the Joint Chiefs of Staff, GCCs may place SOF units under the control of a non-US multinational force commander. In such instances, OPCON of US SOF units will be retained by a US SOF commander within the multinational command structure.

3. Command and Control of Special Operations Forces in Theater

C2 of SOF normally should be executed within a SOF chain of command. C2 of MISO and CA forces will usually be through the SOF chain of command unless the force has been attached to a CF for a specific period or to perform a specific function. The identification of a C2 organizational structure for SOF should depend upon specific objectives, security requirements, and the operational environment. C2 of SOF is executed through one or more of the following:

a. **Theater Special Operations Command.** To provide the necessary unity of command, each GCC (except Commander, US Northern Command) has established a TSOC as a subunified command within their geographic combatant command. US Northern Command maintains an SO division within its operations directorate that serves as a theater SO advisor to the commander. The TSOC is the primary theater SOF organization capable of performing broad continuous missions uniquely suited to SOF capabilities. The TSOC is also the primary mechanism by which a GCC exercises C2 over SOF. The TSOC commander has three principal roles.

(1) **Joint Force Commander.** As the commander of a subunified command, the CDRTSOC is a JFC. As such, he has the authority to plan and conduct joint operations as directed by the GCC and exercises OPCON of assigned commands and forces and normally over attached forces as well. The CDRTSOC may establish JTFs that report directly to him, such as a JSOTF, joint civil-military operations task force (JCMOTF), or JMISOTF, in order to plan and execute these missions.

(2) **Theater SO Advisor.** The CDRTSOC **advises** the GCC, Service component commanders, and designated functional component commanders on the **proper employment of SOF.** The CDRTSOC may develop specific recommendations for the assignment of SOF in theater and opportunities for SOF to support the overall theater campaign plan. The role of theater SO advisor is best accomplished when the GCC establishes the CDRTSOC as a special staff officer on the theater staff (in addition to his duties as a commander—i.e., "dual hatted"). In this case, the CDRTSOC may appoint a deputy as his representative to the theater staff for routine day-to-day staff matters.

(3) **Joint Force Special Operations Component Commander.** When designated by the GCC, the CDRTSOC will function as a JFSOCC. This will normally be the case when the GCC establishes functional component commanders for operations, absent the establishment of a JTF. The CDRTSOC can also be designated the JFSOCC within a JTF if the scope of the operations warrant it (see Figure III-2).

b. Within a GCC's area of responsibility (AOR), there may be several different command relationships regarding SOF. The JFC who is the establishing authority must designate appropriate command relationships among the SOF commanders, CJTFs, and Service and functional component commanders.

(1) The GCC may directly exercise OPCON over one or more JSOTF.

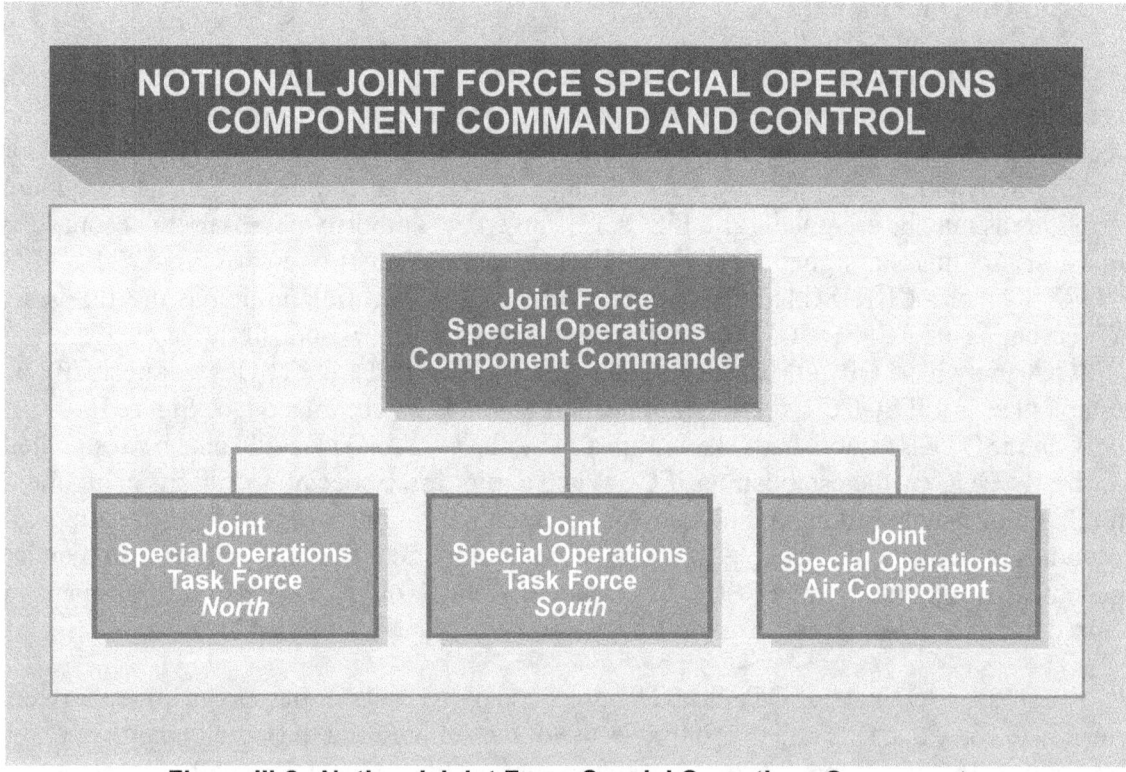

Figure III-2. Notional Joint Force Special Operations Component Command and Control

(2) Typically, a GCC will designate a CDRTSOC or a JFSOCC to exercise OPCON over one or more JSOTFs.

(3) A JFC, subordinate to the GCC (i.e., a CJTF), may have one or more JSOTFs. In this case the JFC would exercise OPCON through a commander, joint special operations task force (CDRJSOTF) or may establish/designate a JFSOCC to exercise OPCON over multiple JSOTFs.

(4) A CDRJSOTF may exercise OPCON over subordinate special operations task forces (SOTFs), and a CDRJSOTF typically exercises OPCON over their assigned SOF and OPCON or TACON of attached SOF.

(5) For the purpose of a C2 discussion a JMISOTF and a JCMOTF should be considered in the same context as a JSOTF for establishing command relationships. However, JMISOTFs and JCMOTFs may include both SOF units and CF units which should be a consideration for the JFC when establishing command relationships.

See JP 3-57, Joint Civil-Military Operations, *for additional details regarding CA, JCMOTFs, and CMO, and JP 3-13.2,* Military Information Support Operations, *for additional details regarding JMISOTFs.*

c. **SOF Operational C2**

(1) **JFSOCC.** The JFSOCC is the commander within a unified command, subordinate unified command, or JTF responsible to the establishing commander for making recommendations on the proper employment of assigned, attached, and/or made available for tasking SOF and assets; planning and coordinating SO; or accomplishing such operational missions as may be assigned. The JFSOCC is given the authority necessary to accomplish missions and tasks assigned by the establishing commander (i.e., a GCC or CJTF). The CDRTSOC or a CDRJSOTF will normally be the individual functioning as the JFSOCC. When acting as a JFSOCC, they retain their authority and responsibilities as JFCs. A JFSOCC may have OPCON over one or more JSOTFs. The CDRTSOC will normally be established as a JFSOCC if there is more than one JSOTF to command (see Figure III-2). If only one JSOTF is established (i.e., within a JTF), the CDRJSOTF could also be designated as the JFSOCC by the establishing JFC. When a joint force special operations component (JFSOC) is established and combined with elements from one or more foreign nations, it becomes a combined forces special operations component (SOC), and its commander becomes a combined forces SOC commander, who would likely control or manage employment of those elements in unified action.

(2) **JSOTF.** A JSOTF is a JTF composed of SO units from more than one Service, formed to carry out a specific SO or prosecute SO in support of a theater campaign or other operations. A JSOTF may have CF tasked to support the conduct of specific missions.

(a) A JSOTF, like any JTF, is normally established by a JFC (e.g., a GCC, a subordinate unified commander such as a CDRTSOC, or a CJTF). For example, a GCC could establish a JTF to conduct operations in a specific joint operations area of the theater. Then either the GCC or the CJTF could establish a JSOTF, subordinate to that JTF, to plan and execute SO. Likewise, a CDRTSOC could establish a JSOTF to focus on a specific mission or operational area assigned by the GCC. A JSOTF may also be established as a joint organization and deployed as an entity from outside the theater, in coordination with that GCC.

(b) A JSOTF is established to conduct operations in a specific operational area or to accomplish a specific mission. If geographically oriented, multiple JSOTFs will normally be assigned different operational areas (e.g., separate JSOAs).

(c) When a JSOTF is formed to directly support a GCC, the CDRTSOC normally acts as the CDRJSOTF. Regardless of whom it is, a CDRJSOTF is a JFC and exercises the authority and responsibility assigned by the establishing authority. A JSOTF staff is normally drawn from the TSOC staff or an existing O-6 level HQ from an existing SOF component with augmentation from other SOF or conventional units and/or personnel as appropriate.

(d) When a JSOTF is established and combined with elements from one or more foreign countries, it typically becomes a combined JSOTF and its commander becomes a combined CDRJSOTF.

For further detailed information on a JSOTF, refer to JP 3-05.1, Joint Special Operations Task Force Operations.

   d. **SOF Subordinate C2 Organizations.** A JSOTF, by its joint designation, has SOF from more than one of the Services: Army special operations forces (ARSOF), Navy special operations forces (NAVSOF), Air Force special operations forces (AFSOF), or Marine Corps special operations forces (MARSOF), and these designations typically denote their forces and subordinate units, not an HQ. In the context of generic Service SOC HQ, they are the Army special operations component (ARSOC), Navy special operations component (NAVSOC), the Air Force special operations component (AFSOC), and the Marine Corps special operations command (MARSOC), respectively. Normally, the only SOF functional component under a CDRTSOC/JFSOCC/CDRJSOTF is a joint special operations air component (JSOAC). A notional depiction of a JSOAC under a JFSOCC is shown in Figure III-2, and a notional depiction of JSOTF elements (including a JSOAC) is shown in Figure III-3.

      (1) **ARSOF.** The ARSOC, as the Army Service force component of a JSOTF, is usually designated as a SOTF and consists of one or more of the following forces: SF, Rangers, and Army special operations aviation (Army SOA). The SOTF is normally commanded and manned by an SF or a Ranger battalion commander and staff. The SOTF normally has MISO and CA forces if they are not part of a separate JMISOTF or JCMOTF, respectively.

         (a) **SOTF.** If there is an SF group or SF battalion, or the Ranger Regiment in the tasked ARSOF, it may be designated a SOTF. The CDRJSOTF may establish multiple subordinate SOTFs, with each SOTF organized around the nucleus of an SF or Ranger unit and may include a mix of ARSOF units and their support elements. The CDRJSOTF may assign each SOTF an area within the JSOA or a functional mission.

         (b) **Special Forces.** SF units are task-organized as SF groups and battalions, both of which have organic HQ and support elements. When deployed, an SF group or battalion may be designated a SOTF.

         (c) **Rangers.** The C2 of Rangers normally is exercised through command posts collocated with other SOF or conventional units. They do not have the organic capability to establish their own forward operations bases. If the Ranger Regiment is deployed, it will normally form a SOTF.

         (d) **Army SOA.** The Army SOA are organic ARSOF assets with OPCON normally exercised by the CDRJSOTF through either the Service component, ARSOC, commander, or a joint special operations air component commander (JSOACC), depending on the situation. For example, when a JSOACC is established as a functional component commander by the CDRTSOC/JFSOCC/CDRJSOTF, the Army SOA may be under TACON, or tasked in support of the JSOACC.

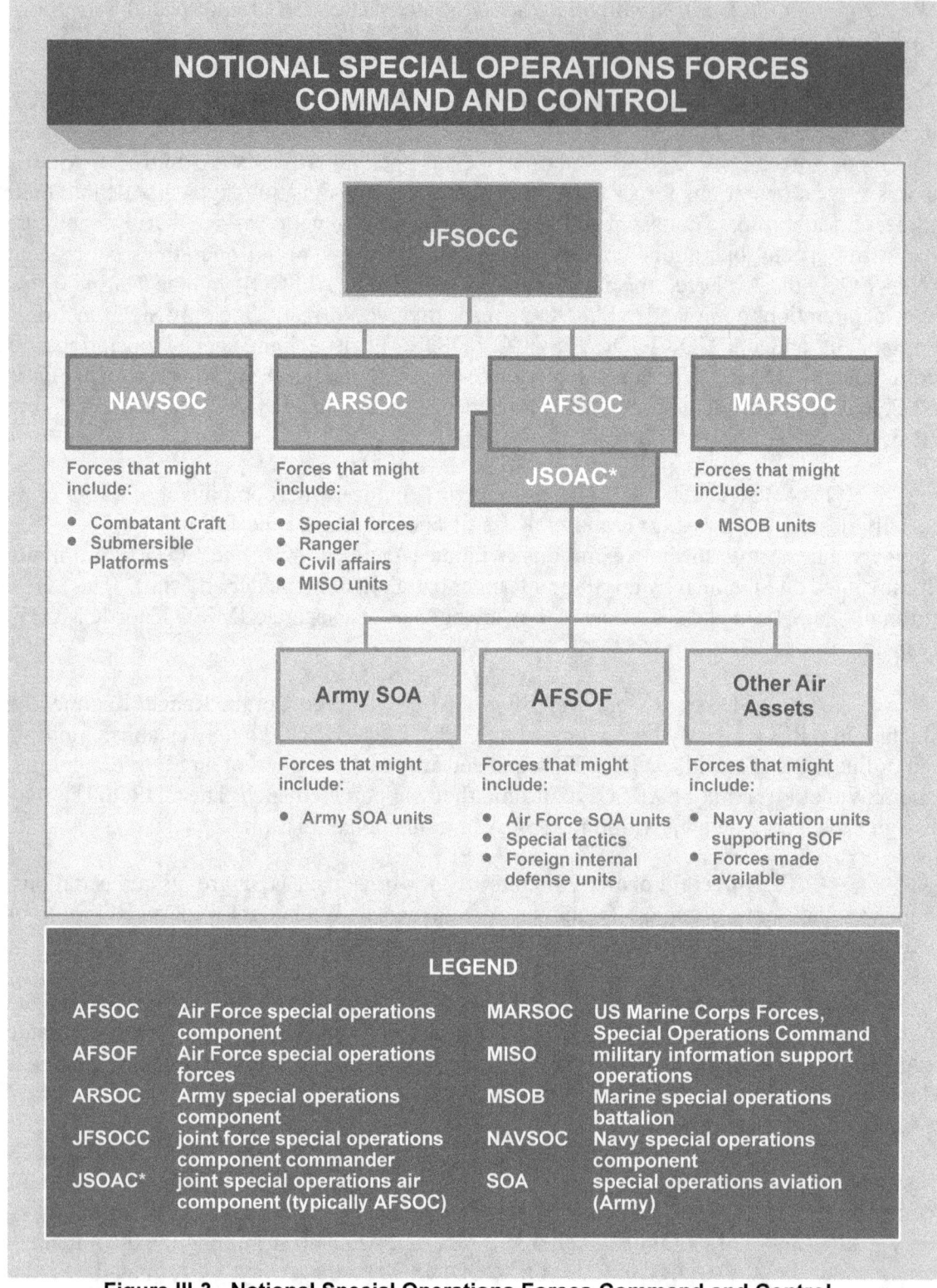

Figure III-3. Notional Special Operations Forces Command and Control

(2) **NAVSOF.** The NAVSOC task organization is based on operational requirements. The NAVSOC may include SEALs, submersible platforms, combatant craft, and supporting forces.

(a) Naval Special Warfare Task Force. For a major operation or campaign, the NAVSOC is referred to as a naval special warfare task force (NSWTF) and is commanded by a SEAL captain (O-6). An NSWTF has one or more subordinate naval special warfare task groups (NSWTGs).

(b) NSWTG. The NAVSOC may be an NSWTG commanded by a SEAL commander (O-5). An NSWTG has one or more subordinate naval special warfare task units (NSWTUs).

(3) **AFSOF.** The AFSOC (not to be confused with the Air Force Special Operations Command that is the Air Force component of USSOCOM) is the Air Force component, normally composed of a special operations wing, special operations group, or squadron, and an element of an Air Force special tactics group. A JSOACC, if designated by the JFSOCC/CDRJSOTF, is typically the AFSOC commander. When subordinate AFSOF units deploy to forward operations bases or advanced operations bases, the AFSOC commander may establish one or more provisional units as follows:

(a) **Air Force Special Operations Detachment (AFSOD).** The AFSOD is a squadron-size AFSOF HQ that could be a composite organization composed of different US Air Force assets. The AFSOD normally is subordinate to an AFSOC, JSOAC, JSOTF, or a JTF depending upon the size and duration of the operation, and the joint organizational structure.

(b) **Air Force Special Operations Element (AFSOE).** The AFSOE contains selected AFSOF units that are normally subordinate to an AFSOC or AFSOD.

(4) **MARSOF.** MARSOC is the Marine Corps Service component of USSOCOM. Although MARSOC HQ is nondeployable, when tasked by CDRUSSOCOM, MARSOC units deploy as needed in support of USSOCOM to form, deploy, and employ a JSOTF. The MARSOF of a JSOTF may be one of the following subordinate commands.

(a) **Marine SO Battalions.** There are three Marine SO line battalions, each with four companies. These companies can be task organized to conduct SR, DA, SFA, and FID missions in support of USSOCOM or a supported GCC, whether under a CDRJSOTF or a CJTF. These companies may also provide tailored military combat skills training and advisor support for identified foreign forces.

(b) **Marine SO Support Group.** It provides specified support capabilities for SO missions as directed by the MARSOC.

(5) **JSOAC.** JSOAC collectively refers to the commander, staff, and assets of a SO functional air component of a subordinate unified command, a JFSOC or a JSOTF. A CDRTSOC/JFSOCC/CDRJSOTF may designate a JSOACC to be responsible for the centralized planning and direction and the execution of joint SO air activities, and for coordinating conventional air support for the SOF with the JFC's designated joint force air component commander (JFACC). The JSOACC will normally be the commander with the preponderance of air assets and/or the greatest ability to plan, coordinate, allocate, task, control, and support the assigned/supporting air assets. There may be circumstances when

the SOF commander may elect to place selected SO aviation assets under separate control. A JSOACC may be subordinate to a single CDRJSOTF or tasked to support multiple CDRJSOTFs within a JFSOC (see Figure III-2). A JSOAC may be a standing organization or can be formed in response to a contingency or other operation.

4. Special Operations Forces as the Lead for a Joint Task Force

With the increased IW nature of operations and a whole-of-government effort in unified action to defeat global, networked, and transnational irregular adversaries, there may be cases where the C2 construct based on *preponderance of forces* may not be the primary consideration in establishing a JTF. In some cases, a C2 construct based on *SO expertise and influence* may be better suited to the overall conduct of an operation (i.e., superiority in the aggregate of applicable capabilities, experience, specialized equipment, and knowledge of and relationships with relevant populations), with the JTF being built around a core SO staff. Such a JTF has both SOF and CF and the requisite ability to command and control them. SOF and their unique capabilities are particularly well-suited for such complex situations because of their regional familiarity, language and cultural awareness, and understanding of the social dynamics within and among the relevant populations (i.e., tribal politics, social networks, religious influences, and customs and mores). SOF also maintain special relationships with other participants within unified action. Given the SOF expertise and the special operations form of "maneuver," SOF may be best suited to lead US forces in some operational areas. Accordingly, an optimal construct can be one having a SOF chain of command supported by CF and their enabling functions. **Such a construct calls for a SOF JFC, not as a JFSOCC/CDRJSOTF, but as the CJTF.**

a. **TSOC-Based JTF.** An example of this C2 construct is a JTF staff built around a TSOC, integrating SOF and CF with appropriate enabling functions. If needed, the TSOC can be enhanced by a deployable joint task force augmentation cell (DJTFAC). CDRUSSOCOM maintains a DJTFAC, currently identified as *JTF Sword*—a joint, multi-disciplined group of SO planners and staff experts capable of establishing a SOF C2 element or integrating with a forming or formed SOF HQ to rapidly establish a JTF HQ providing C2 for conducting operations within IW. USSOCOM also has a robust global reach-back capability for additional SOF, staff expertise, and special operations-peculiar (SO-peculiar) support. SO-peculiar support is explained in Chapter IV, "Support Considerations for Special Operations Forces."

b. **USSOCOM JTF.** Another example is a unique JTF resourced by and under the C2 of CDRUSSOCOM. The USSOCOM JTF, currently identified as *JTF 487,* is a separately established, deployable, scalable, senior-level HQ that can take command of a complex "direct-indirect" force structure in ambiguous conflict environments to conduct operations within IW. This JTF is not built around a TSOC, nor does it compete with an Army corps or TSOC; however, it can integrate with an established HQ, and can augment a TSOC or other deployed organization. Additionally, the USSOCOM JTF provides a minimal footprint and streamlined leadership hierarchy, using the USSOCOM Global Mission Support Center—a single point of entry providing SOF customers a reach-back, push-forward, and think-ahead capability for operational and emerging requirements.

5. Integration and Interoperability of Conventional Forces and Special Operations Forces

SOF and CF often share the same operational environment for extended periods. While SOF-CF integration poses challenges, there are also great opportunities the JFC may exploit. This integration often creates additional options for achieving objectives. Integration and interoperability enable the JFC to take advantage of both SOF and CF core competencies and Service or SOF unique systems. Effective SOF-CF integration facilitates the synchronizing of military operations in time, space, and purpose; maximizes the capability of the joint force; allows the JFC to optimize the principles of joint operations in planning and execution; and may produce an operating tempo and battle rhythm with which the enemy is unable to cope. It may also reduce the potential for fratricide. Accordingly, focus should be placed on three key areas: operations, command relationships, and liaisons.

a. Operations

(1) As CF now perform some traditional SOF roles, such as providing advisor teams to FSF, it is especially important that SOF and CF start planning and integrating operations, beginning with the first efforts at mission development and concluding with the achievement of the desired end state.

(2) SOF and CF units should integrate early, prior to deployments, to build and foster relationships, understand each others' planning processes, and defuse any misconceptions or friction points. When possible, units should attend training events together, exchange briefings on capabilities and limitations, and coordinate staff actions.

(3) During operations, SOF and CF commanders should understand each other's mission planning cycles, intelligence and operations cycles, and mission approval processes. Mission type orders (task and purpose) are optimal to convey the commander's intent to permit flexibility, initiative, and responsiveness.

b. Command Relationships

(1) Properly established and clearly articulated command relationships can directly support decentralization (i.e., decentralized planning and execution for individual missions), foster trust, and aid synergy. These command relationships can broaden the mindset from a very "vertical" focus on receiving and accomplishing activities from the higher commander to a "horizontal" focus, working much more closely with partners.

(2) Successful execution of SO requires clear, responsive C2 by an appropriate SOF C2 element. The limited window of opportunity normally associated with the majority of SOF missions, as well as the sensitive nature of many of these missions, requires a C2 structure that is responsive to the needs of the operational unit. As will be covered in Chapter IV, "Support Considerations for Special Operations Forces," SOF C2 may be uniquely tailored for a specific mission or operation.

c. Liaisons.
Liaison between SOF and all components of the joint force is essential for effective force employment to coordinate, synchronize, and deconflict SO with CF

operations—effective liaison can prevent fratricide, maximize opportunities, and ensure mutual understanding.

For further information on CF-SOF integration and interoperability, refer to USSOCOM Publication 3-33, v.3, CF/SOF Multi-Service Tactics, Techniques, and Procedures for Conventional Forces and Special Operations Forces Integration and Interoperability, *and JP 3-05.1*, Joint Special Operations Task Force Operations.

6. Coordination and Liaison Elements

SOF commanders have specific elements that facilitate liaison and coordination. They include the special operations command and control element (SOCCE) to command and control, and coordinate SOF activities with CF; the special operations liaison element (SOLE) to provide liaison to the JFACC or appropriate Service component air C2 facility; and SOF liaison officers (LNOs) placed in a variety of locations as necessary to coordinate, synchronize, and deconflict SO within the operational area. All of these elements significantly improve the flow of information, facilitate concurrent planning, and enhance overall mission accomplishment of the joint force.

a. **SOCCE.** The SOCCE is the focal point for the synchronization of SOF activities with conventional force operations. It performs C2 or liaison functions according to mission requirements and as directed by the establishing SOF commander (JFSOCC or CDRJSOTF as appropriate). Its level of authority and responsibility may vary widely. The SOCCE normally is employed when SOF conduct operations in support of a conventional force. It collocates with the command post of the supported force to coordinate, synchronize, and deconflict SO with the operations of the supported force and to ensure communications interoperability with that force. The SOCCE can receive SOF operational, intelligence, and target acquisition reports directly from deployed SOF elements and provide them to the supported component HQ. The JFSOCC, CDRJSOTF, or JSOTF component commanders may attach liaison teams from other SOF elements to the SOCCE as required. The SOCCE remains under the OPCON of the establishing SOF commander. The SOCCE performs the following functions:

(1) As directed, facilitates or exercises C2 of SOF tactical elements attached to, or placed in direct support of, the supported CF commander.

(2) Advises the CF commander on the current situation, missions, capabilities, and limitations of supporting and supported SOF units.

(3) Advises the supporting SOF commander(s) of the supported force commander's current situation, missions, intentions, and requirements.

(4) Provides required secure communications links.

(5) Coordinates and deconflicts SO activities with operations of the CF.

(6) When linkup between SOF and CF becomes imminent, assists the supported CF commander and staff with SOF linkup planning and execution.

b. **SOLE.** A SOLE is typically a joint team provided by the JFSOCC to the JFACC (if designated) or appropriate Service component air C2 organization, to coordinate, deconflict, and integrate special operations air, surface, and subsurface operations with conventional air operations. The SOLE director works directly for the JFSOCC/CDRJSOTF as a liaison and has no command authority for mission tasking, planning, and execution. The SOLE director places SOF ground, maritime, and air liaison personnel in the joint air operations center (JAOC) to coordinate, deconflict, and synchronize SOF with conventional air operations. The SOLE also provides coordination for the visibility of SOF operations in the air tasking order and the airspace control order. The SOLE must also coordinate appropriate fire support coordination measures between the JAOC and the SOF HQ to help prevent potential for fratricide. A SOLE is tailored as appropriate (see Figure III-4).

c. **SOF LNOs.** SOF LNOs report to the SOF commander or SOF component commander and are dispatched to applicable conventional JTF components to ensure the timely exchange of necessary operational and support information to aid mission execution and preclude fratricide, duplication of effort, disruption of ongoing operations, or loss of intelligence sources. SOF LNOs may assist in the coordination of fire support, overflight, aerial refueling, targeting, deception, MISO, CAO, and other operational issues based on current and future SO missions. These efforts are crucial to the JFC's unity of effort, tempo, and coordination of limited resources and assets.

7. Joint Special Operations Area

a. Coordination and deconfliction with CF are always critical concerns for SOF commanders. SOF are often employed prior to the arrival of CF. Effective coordination is vital in the transition from advance force operations involving SOF to follow-on operations and in ensuring that the timing and tempo of the overall campaign is maintained.

b. The **JFC may establish a JSOA,** which is a restricted area of land, sea, and airspace assigned by a JFC to the commander of a joint special operations force to conduct SO activities. The commander of SOF may further assign a specific area or sector within the JSOA to a subordinate commander for mission execution. The scope and duration of the SOF mission, friendly and hostile situation, and politico-military considerations all influence the number, composition, and sequencing of SOF deployed into a JSOA. It may be limited in size to accommodate a discrete DA mission or may be extensive enough to allow a continuing broad range of UW operations. JFCs may use a JSOA to delineate and facilitate simultaneous use of CF and SOF in the same general operational area. When a JSOA is designated, the JFSOCC (or CDRJSOTF) is the supported commander within the designated JSOA.

c. Establishment of a designated JSOA for SOF to conduct unilateral operations assists in the ease of control of SO and the prevention of fratricide.

NOTIONAL SPECIAL OPERATIONS LIAISON ELEMENT FUNCTIONS

SOLE Director: Liaison to JFACC

Strategy Division
- Coordinates and synchronizes SO strategy and targets with other components to meet combatant commander objectives and guidance.
- Nominate SOF targets for inclusion in the joint integrated prioritized target list.
- Provides SOF input for JFC apportionment recommendation decisions.

Combat Plans Division
- Coordinates SOF air requirements within the master air attack plan.
- Coordinates with JSOTF/JSOAC on ATO inputs and ensures distributed ATOs are merged with the master ATO.
- Provides SO input for inclusion in SPINS.
- Coordinates airspace requirements and deconfliction for future operations.
- Represents the SO components on the targeting effects team in the JAOC.

Combat Operations Division
- Monitors and coordinates current day flying operations with other components.
- Deconflicts ongoing SO surface operations in real time with other components.
- Maintains updated list of team locations for deconfliction.
- Coordinates support for and prosecution of SOF-monitored targets to include time-sensitive targets.
- Coordinates airspace management with JAOC airspace manager.

Intelligence, Surveillance, and Reconnaissance Division
- Coordinates ISR requirements for SOF in the field.
- Provides intelligence support for combat plans and operations division.

Other Coordination
- Coordinates requirements for airfield surveys supporting force basing (AMD).
- Coordinates JTAC support for SOF when required.
- Coordinates logistic requirements including supply, transportation, and contracting (AMD).
- Coordinates communications requirements, as necessary, for SOF in the field (communications representative).
- Coordinates with JPRC.

LEGEND

AMD	air mobility division	JSOAC	joint special operations air component
ATO	air tasking order		
ISR	intelligence, surveillance, and reconnaissance	JSOTF	joint special operations task force
		JTAC	joint terminal attack controller
JAOC	joint air operations center	SO	special operations
JFACC	joint force air component commander	SOF	special operations forces
JFC	joint force commander	SOLE	special operations liaison element
JPRC	joint personnel recovery center	SPINS	special instructions

Figure III-4. Notional Special Operations Liaison Element Functions

8. Interorganizational Coordination

a. Interagency coordination is as integral to SO as it is conventional operations, and fostering personal relationships between SOF commanders and interorganizational leaders and professional relations between both staffs should be a routine objective during military engagement activities.

b. A proven model in attaining unity of effort with interorganizational partners is the complementary character of the DOS embassy mission strategic plans and country operational plans, and a GCC's theater campaign plan.

c. Interpersonal communication skills that emphasize consultation, persuasion, compromise, and consensus are the means to obtain unified action in a military-civilian effort. Successful commanders and staff build personal relationships to inspire trust and confidence. The challenges of gaining harmony and creating synergy among the engaged USG agencies and multinational partners are greater as there are no clear authorities directing the relationship. If tasked by the GCC/CJTF, a CDRJSOTF may be the coordinating authority for some form of interorganizational coordination at what could be characterized as the operational level, and responsible for the unified action down through the tactical level.

For further information on interagency considerations, refer to JP 3-08, Interorganizational Coordination During Joint Operations.

9. Multinational Coordination

SOF operate with multinational forces (MNFs), i.e., forces belonging to a coalition or alliance, on a routine and recurring basis. US SOF assess, train, advise, assist, and operate with a plethora of multinational foreign special operations units. They also do the same with many multinational conventional force units, in both supported and supporting relationships.

a. SOF training or operating with MNFs is typically the result of tasking by a CCDR in coordination with the appropriate DOS representatives and other interagency partners. Coordination of national level direction among the MNF partners should be anticipated at the national and theater levels.

b. **Command Considerations.** Any control of SOF operating elements transferred to a foreign commander must include an appropriate SOF command element in the chain of command for direct C2 of the SOF operating elements.

c. For MNF operations, rules of engagement (ROE) may be different for the non-US military units, than for US units. That could result in some form of operating limitations. US military forces may have to follow more restrictive ROE (US or multinational) dependent upon agreed command relationships; however, they always retain their right to self-defense per US ROE. ROE typically is coordinated with all MNF participants. US ROE must be coordinated by the supported JFC.

d. SOF may be tasked to liaise with and advise units of a MNF, providing the primary means of communications and C2 with the MNF operational HQ. This could mean the SOF would require significant additional communications equipment to facilitate the C2 and coordination responsibilities.

e. MNF operations typically require some degree of US logistics support to be coordinated.

f. Although capable in many foreign languages, for MNF operations the SOF may require interpreters to facilitate communication and coordination.

g. Foreign disclosure will always be a consideration for coordination and release of intelligence and other information.

h. There should be a multinational coordination center, especially if the MNF is operating under a parallel command structure, to facilitate most, if not all coordination efforts among the MNF.

For further information on multinational coordination and operations, refer to JP 3-16, Multinational Operations.

CHAPTER IV
SUPPORT CONSIDERATIONS FOR SPECIAL OPERATIONS FORCES

> *"The operational effectiveness of our deployed forces cannot be, and never has been, achieved without being enabled by our joint Service partners. The support Air Force, Army, Marine, and Navy engineers, [explosive ordnance disposal] technicians, intelligence analysts, and the numerous other professions that contribute to SOF [special operations forces], have substantially increased our capabilities and effectiveness throughout the world."*
>
> **Admiral Eric T. Olson**
> **December 2008**

1. Introduction

SOF support must be tailored to specific mission requirements, yet flexible enough to respond to changing employment parameters. The joint character of SO requires support arrangements across Service lines with emphasis on unique support required in order to sustain independent and remote operations. Further, SOF must be able to exploit information derived from the full range of available multinational, national, theater, and tactical intelligence, surveillance, and reconnaissance support systems.

2. Intelligence Support

All-source, fused intelligence is vital in identifying relevant targets, COA development, and mission planning/execution. SO require detailed planning, often by relatively small units. Consequently, intelligence requirements are normally greater in scope and depth than that of CF. Joint intelligence preparation of the operational environment (JIPOE) provides the foundation for SO intelligence production. Like CF operations, SO intelligence analysis focuses on the operational area and the area of interest (AOI); however, the strategic nature of SO frequently incorporates an expanded AOI. SO planning typically requires a comprehensive analysis of the geopolitical and socioeconomic situation in the operational area and AOI to ensure all factors that may affect mission accomplishment are considered. SO, having a reduced margin of error due to the small size of teams, require greater depth in target intelligence and greater detail in JIPOE to ensure success and avoid casualties.

a. **Interface with National and Theater Intelligence Assets.** The ability to interface with theater/national intelligence systems and assets is critical for SO mission success. The combatant command joint intelligence operations center (JIOC) is the focal point for intelligence activities in support of joint operations with additional support from the Defense Intelligence Operations Coordination Center (DIOCC). Joint force requests for information (RFIs) are forwarded to the combatant command JIOC. If the JIOC is unable to respond, RFIs are forwarded to the DIOCC. The DIOCC will then interface with other DOD intelligence agencies or the national intelligence community through the National Intelligence Coordination Center (NICC) to provide support. If the DIOCC determines that the information required has not been produced by any agency in the intelligence community, the DIOCC will coordinate with the combatant command JIOC and NICC to recommend an appropriate strategy to collect, process, analyze, produce, and disseminate the required information. A JSOTF, when formed, will have access to these same theater and national interfaces through the combatant command JIOC and the DIOCC. Additionally, a JSOTF may be augmented with a national intelligence support team comprised of representatives from many national intelligence and combat support agencies.

b. **All-Source Intelligence.** The nature of many SO objectives and tactics requires all-source intelligence support that is often more detailed than that required in conventional operations. SOF often use intelligence information to avoid adversary forces, regardless of size or composition, as opposed to intelligence information that would allow CF to engage the adversary (see Figure IV-1).

c. **Expanded Focus.** Intelligence support for SOF conducting military engagement, security cooperation, crisis response, or limited contingencies requires various intelligence disciplines to widen their focus. This includes political, informational, economic, and cultural institutions and relationships as well as adversary, friendly force, and target specific data including the use of civil information management and other open-source information avenues. This is particularly true during FID and when tasked to participate in noncombatant evacuation operations.

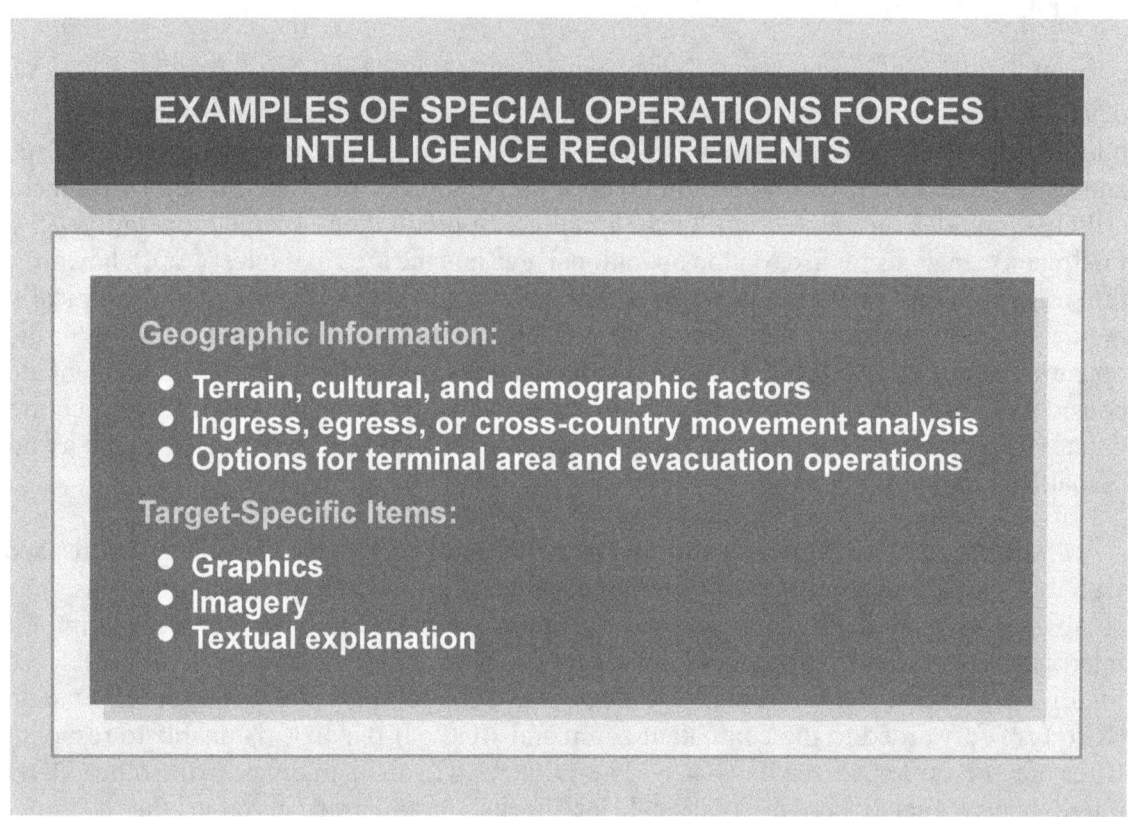

Figure IV-1. Examples of Special Operations Forces Intelligence Requirements

d. **Sensitivity to HN and Adversary Collection Efforts.** SO missions are particularly sensitive to HN and adversary collection efforts. Counterintelligence support and OPSEC assist in protecting sensitive SO missions.

e. **Geospatial Intelligence (GEOINT) Support.** GEOINT support can provide timely, complete, and accurate information to help SOF with the visualization of the operational environment. SOF commanders use GEOINT to help determine friendly and adversary COAs and to plan for deployment of SOF and key weapons systems. GEOINT contingency planning identifies the AOI and determines GEOINT requirements for SO activities and weapons systems. It also determines current availability for resources to meet those requirements, determines risk, and then develops a production strategy to address shortfalls. During crisis action planning (CAP), the requirement to plan GEOINT support for crisis response operations depends greatly upon the scope of the mission, how much GEOINT can be adapted from existing contingency plans, and the total time available for GEOINT to be included in the CAP process. When plans call for working in a multinational force or with HN forces, early consideration should be given to developing and using releasable intelligence products, to the maximum extent consistent with security considerations. This will facilitate a common operational picture.

f. **SOF Support to National and Theater Human Information Requirements.** While SO can be informed by national and theater intelligence assets, SO fill a critical gap in providing information that is not available through technical means. SOF's presence in denied or politically sensitive areas can provide enhanced situational awareness to a JFC that would not otherwise be available.

For further information on intelligence support, refer to JP 2-01, Joint and National Intelligence Support to Military Operations, *JP 2-01.3,* Joint Intelligence Preparation of the Operational Environment, *and JP 3-05.1,* Joint Special Operations Task Force Operations.

For further information on GEOINT, refer to JP 2-03, Geospatial Intelligence Support to Joint Operations.

3. Operational Contract Support

Operational contract support is as integral to SO as it is to conventional operations. The continual introduction of high-tech equipment, coupled with force structure and manning limitations, and high operating tempo mean that SOF may be augmented with contracted support, including contingency contractor employees and all tiers of subcontractor employees who are specifically authorized through their contract to accompany the force and have protected status in accordance with international conventions (i.e., contractors authorized to accompany the force). To do this, contract support integration and contractor management must be integrated into military planning and operations. Early integration of these planning considerations also allows for any unique security clearance or OPSEC concerns related to the SO.

For more information regarding operational contract support, see JP 4-10, Operational Contract Support.

4. Host-Nation Support

Host-nation support (HNS) is that civil and/or military assistance rendered by a nation to foreign forces within its territory based on agreements mutually concluded between nations. For SO, HNS must be weighed against OPSEC considerations, mission requirements and duration, and the operational environment. HNS is a key common-user logistics area of concern.

a. HNS may often play an important role in reducing the military logistic footprint in theater, thus allowing the deployment of increased combat capabilities early in the operation. HNS can also provide long-term logistic support, thus freeing up key military logistic capabilities for other contingencies.

b. Some considerations for HNS:

(1) Authority for negotiations must be obtained through the supported JFC (to include the supported GCC) and through the appropriate US COM channels.

(2) Whenever possible, HNS agreements should include the authority for the CDRJSOTF to coordinate directly with the HN for support, acquisition, and use of facilities and real estate.

(3) Every effort should be made to obtain language support for negotiations with local nationals.

(4) A legal advisor experienced in HNS should be involved in the HNS agreements process.

(5) It is critical to determine a lead agency to contract and negotiate HNS.

(6) To optimize effective HNS, there should be centralized planning and coordination of HNS functions (i.e., identification of requirements and procurement).

(7) Especially for SOF, the movement/distribution and security of applicable HNS items must be considered, based on the operational environment.

For additional information regarding HNS, see JP 3-05.1, Joint Special Operations Task Force Operations, *and JP 4-0,* Joint Logistics. *Refer to DODD 2010.9,* Acquisition and Cross-Servicing Agreements, *for policy for the acquisition from and transfer to authorized foreign governments of logistics support, supplies, and services.*

5. Logistic Support

GCCs and their Service component commanders, in coordination with the CDRTSOC, are responsible for ensuring that effective and responsive support systems are developed and provided for assigned/attached SOF. The CDRTSOC, or the JFSOCC/CDRJSOTF, when a JTF is established, validates logistic requirements for SOF in theater for the GCC. To the extent possible, SOF logistic requirements should be identified during the contingency planning process. Logistic support for SOF units can be provided through one or more of the following:

a. **Service Support.** The logistic support of SOF units is the responsibility of their parent Service, except where otherwise provided for by support agreements or other directives. This responsibility exists regardless of whether the SOF unit requiring support is assigned to the Service component, the TSOC, JFSOCC, or a JSOTF. SOF Service-common logistic support includes equipment, material, supplies, and services adopted by a military Service for use by its own forces and their activities. These include standard military items, base operating support, and the supplies and services provided by a Service to support and sustain its own forces, including those forces assigned to the combatant commands. Items and services defined as Service-common by one Service are not necessarily Service-common for all other Services.

b. **Joint In-Theater Support.** The majority of SOF missions require joint logistic planning and execution. When a theater Service component cannot satisfy its Service SOF support requirements, the GCC will determine if another Service component can do so through common or joint servicing arrangements. Joint logistic arrangements may also be used when more effective than normal Service support.

c. **Nonstandard Support.** When operations involving SOF impose time, geographic, and/or resource constraints on the theater support infrastructure, making it impractical for the theater to provide the requisite support to SOF, the GCC may request from CDRUSSOCOM the deployment of organic USSOCOM combat service support assets.

d. **SO-Peculiar Support.** SO-peculiar logistic support includes equipment, materials, supplies, and services required for SO missions for which there is no Service-common requirement. These are limited to items and services initially designed for, or used by, SOF until adopted for Service-common use by one or more Service. Modifications are approved by CDRUSSOCOM for application to standard items and services used by the Services, and items and services identified as critically urgent for the immediate accomplishment of a special operations mission. This support will be provided via USSOCOM Service component logistic infrastructures and in coordination with theater Service components.

e. **HNS.** Countries with or without a government infrastructure may only be able to provide limited logistics support.

For further information on SOF logistic support, refer to JP 4-0, Joint Logistics, and JP 3-05.1, Joint Special Operations Task Force Operations.

6. Health Service Support

SOF teams frequently operate in remote areas and therefore, are exposed to health threats not normally seen in the other areas of the respective HNs. As a consequence, proactive force health protection is critical for mission success and preservation of high-value SOF assets. SOF will often operate in theaters that are underdeveloped with little or no health care support structure. Point-to-point movement to designated Medical Treatment

Facilities is standard while medical regulating and strategic aeromedical evacuation (AE) might be required and should be part of the contingency planning process.

a. **Austere SOF Support Structure.** SOF health service support is characterized by an austere structure and a limited number of medical personnel with enhanced medical skills. SOF medical personnel often provide emergency treatment and a basic level of medical care at the operational team level with organic medical assets. Additional medical support and patient movement (see Figure IV-2) provided to SOF units in the operational area can be planned and conducted by SOF medical personnel. Not all SOF missions require SOF-trained medical assets. SOF medical assets are limited and may require support from conventional units. Casualty evacuation (CASEVAC) for SOF personnel is the transport of casualties by any expedient means possible. SOF medical personnel perform CASEVAC missions, forward of the intermediate staging base (ISB), on opportune aircraft or other means of transport, back to the ISB or a predetermined point where AE assets are located. Requests for medical regulating should be submitted to the appropriate patient movement requirements center after competent medical authority attests to the need to move the patient. AE is conducted once the casualty is regulated into the patient movement system. AE is performed using fixed-wing aircraft and AE trained medical crews. It is the movement of patients under medical supervision to and between medical treatment facilities. SOF units have varying degrees of first responder (Role 1) capabilities and limited forward resuscitative (Role 2) capabilities. SOF do not have organic theater hospitalization (Role 3) or definitive care (Role 4) capabilities readily available to them and must rely on either available theater health service support assets or local HN capabilities when access to theater hospitalization (Role 3) care is an urgent necessity.

b. **Conventional Support Structure.** Provision of medical support beyond SOF capabilities depends on the thoroughness of advanced planning so that the conventional medical support structure umbrella is extended to cover the limited organic capability or to meet requirements for additional medical assets (such as surgical intervention, evacuation, and expanded medical logistics). SOF medical units deploy with initial assets to support operational planning requirements. Deployed medical resupply is the responsibility of the theater medical logistics system. SOF and theater medical planners need to establish a responsive medical logistics resupply process utilizing the theater medical logistics system. Certain operations may also require special security requirements to be put in place to not compromise the identification of SOF personnel upon entry into the conventional medical system.

For further information on health service support, refer to JP 4-02, Health Service Support, *and JP 3-05.1,* Joint Special Operations Task Force Operations.

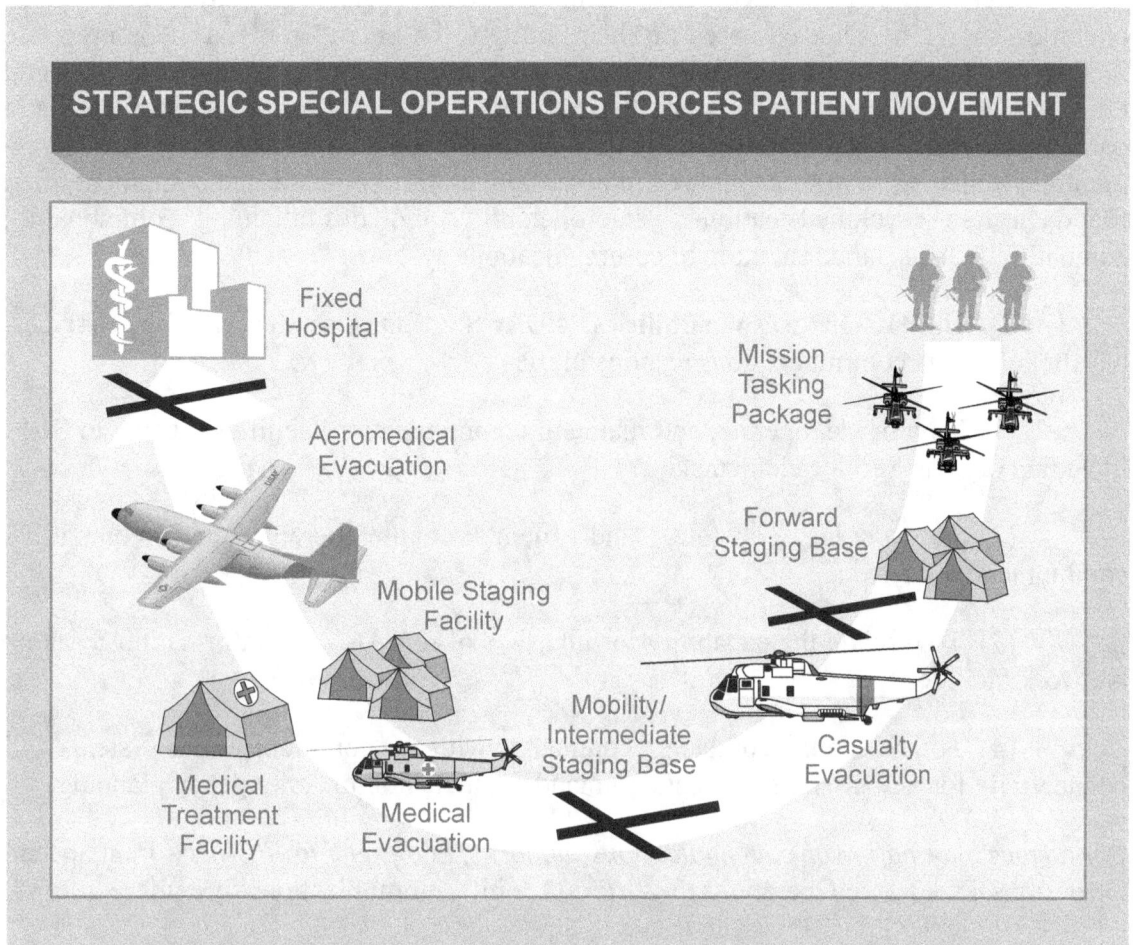

Figure IV-2. Strategic Special Operations Forces Patient Movement

7. Communications Systems Support

a. **Global Support.** Communications systems support to SOF normally are global, secure, and jointly interoperable. It must be flexible so that it can be tailored to specific SO missions and it must add value to the SOF operational capability. Communications systems support the full range of SO worldwide. SOF must be able to communicate anywhere and anytime using the full range of national capabilities required to support the mission. Therefore, SOF operational units have a variety of methods for communicating, reporting, and querying available resources, regardless of geographic location.

b. **Multiple and Varied Systems.** SOF communications support consists of multiple and varied groups of systems, procedures, personnel, and equipment that operate in diverse manners and at different echelons, from the national to the tactical levels. Communications systems have to support discrete as well as collective functions. SOF missions are normally controlled at the lowest operational level that can accomplish the needed coordination, although political considerations may require control at the national level. SOF communications systems are set up to offer seamless connectivity.

c. **Interoperable Systems.** SOF communications systems employed for a given operation should be selected based on their ability to be interoperable at the appropriate security level with the systems deployed by US CF, joint commands, multinational units, and US commercial networks to facilitate the seamless transport of critical information and common services. They should also have the flexibility to integrate not only with state-of-the-art systems, but also be capable of integrating with less sophisticated equipment often found in less developed nations. Interoperability includes attaining commonality, compatibility, and standardization of communications systems.

d. **CDRUSSOCOM Responsibilities.** CDRUSSOCOM, as do each of the Services, has the following communications responsibilities:

(1) To provide, operate, and maintain communication facilities organic to SOF, including organic Service elements.

(2) To provide, operate, and maintain interoperable and compatible communications systems.

(3) To provide the capability for interface of non-Defense Information Systems Network facilities.

(4) To provide the combatant commands with SO communications systems and connectivity for SOF assigned to that command for inclusion in contingency planning.

For further information on communications support of SOF, refer to JP 3-05.1, Joint Special Operations Task Force Operations, *and JP 6-0,* Joint Communications System.

8. Public Affairs Support

a. **Diplomatic and Political Sensitivity of SO.** The diplomatic and political sensitivity of many SO mandates that thorough and accurate PA guidance be developed during the operational planning stage and approved for use in advance of most SO.

b. **Accurate Reflection of the SO Mission.** PA planning must accurately reflect the objective of the mission to domestic audiences consistent with the overall MISO and CMO effort, and with strategic, operational, and tactical OPSEC requirements. The commander should develop proposed PA guidance that is coordinated with supporting commands and government agencies, as appropriate, prior to forwarding that guidance to the Assistant Secretary of Defense (Public Affairs) for approval.

For further information on PA support, refer to JP 3-61, Public Affairs, *and JP 3-05.1,* Joint Special Operations Task Force Operations.

9. Combat Camera Support

a. **Combat camera** provides still and video documentary products that support MISO and other SO missions. Many combat camera teams supporting SOF are specially equipped with night vision and digital image transmission capabilities. Combat camera also provides gun camera image processing for theater and national use. Combat camera imagery is used to portray the true nature of US operations to multinational partners and civilian populaces, as well as adversaries, and to counter adversary disinformation with on-screen or gun camera evidence. The SOF link to combat camera support normally is through the supported GCC's IO cell and the visual information planner.

b. **Visual Information.** The coordination of visual information is an important function that leverages this extensive cross-element support. Each of the following contributes some type of imagery—all of which are combined to shape a comprehensive visualization package for special operations missions. Visual information is derived from a variety of sources such as unmanned aircraft collected imagery, photo journalist collected imagery, PA imagery, intelligence related imagery, satellite imagery, individual soldier collected imagery, gun camera imagery, as well as combat camera products. The visual information function supports the overall planning and implementation of SO and is especially valuable to a commander's communications strategy. The communication strategy is the JFC's strategy for coordinating and synchronizing themes, messages, images, and actions to support objectives and to ensure the integrity and consistency of themes and messages to the lowest tactical level.

10. Legal Support

SO missions frequently involve a unique set of complex issues. There are federal laws and executive orders, federal agency publications and directives, the law of armed conflict, and ROE that may affect SO missions as well as the SO joint planning and targeting processes. These guidelines become especially critical during sensitive contingency missions when international and domestic laws, treaty provisions, and political agreements may affect mission planning and execution. SOF commanders must seek legal review during all levels of planning and execution of SO missions, to include planning of the ROE.

For further information on legal support, refer to JP 1-04, Legal Support, *and JP 3-05.1,* Joint Special Operations Task Force Operations.

11. Protection

a. The protection of the force is an essential consideration. Protection focuses on conserving the SOF fighting potential, whether operating independently, or as part of a larger joint force in a major operation/campaign. The four primary ways: active defensive measures that protect the joint force, its information, its bases, necessary infrastructure, and lines of communications from an adversary's attack; passive defensive measures that make friendly forces, systems, and facilities difficult to locate, strike, and destroy; applying technology and procedures to reduce the risk of fratricide; and emergency management and response to reduce the loss of personnel and capabilities due to accidents, health threats, and natural disasters. As the JFC's mission requires, the protection function also extends beyond force protection to encompass protection of US civilians; the forces, systems, and civil infrastructure of friendly nations; and OGAs, IGOs, and NGOs. For force protection, typically each GCC has TACON of US forces in their AOR.

b. Protection considerations include basic force security; active and passive air and missile defense; OPSEC; computer network defense (CND); information assurance (IA); electronic protection; personnel recovery; CBRN operations; antiterrorism support; combat identification; survivability; safety; and force health protection.

c. SOF planners should ensure their planning and supported theater plans include as adequate provisions for protection as they would for intelligence, sustainment, communications, etc.

For more detailed information regarding protection, see JP 3-0, Joint Operations.

12. Fire Support

SOF may require long-range, surface-based, joint fire support in remote locations or for targets well beyond the land, maritime, and amphibious operational force area of operations. SOF liaison elements coordinate fire support through both external and SOF channels. SOF liaison elements (e.g., SOCCE and SOLE) provide SOF expertise to coordinate, synchronize, and deconflict SOF fire support. Interoperable communications and detailed procedures between fire support providers and SOF operating deep within enemy territory must be considered. Comprehensive fire support planning between SOF and supporting elements will facilitate rapid, responsive, and accurate mission execution.

For further information on fire support, refer to JP 3-09, Joint Fire Support.

13. Air Support

In addition to their organic air capabilities for infiltration, exfiltration, resupply, and precision fire support, SOF often requires conventional air support that requires timely and detailed planning and coordination. Air support is typically provided by the JFACC (or an Air Force component commander), and the JFSOCC/CDRJSOTF normally provides a SOLE to the JFACC at the JAOC. In addition to helping to deconflict and coordinate SO with the JFACC, the SOLE helps coordinate SO requests for air support. Air support can include intelligence, surveillance, and reconnaissance, airlift, close air support, air refueling, EW, etc., and the use of SOF or CF joint terminal attack controllers (JTACs), TACPs, and/or the elements and capabilities of an Air Force air support operations center (ASOC) located with an Army component command. JTACs/TACPs can work directly for SOF units supporting various missions. ASOCs can help the SOF commander integrate and synchronize use of air power to support SO. Elements provided to SOF units may require additional training or equipment to effectively and safely facilitate air support during SO.

14. Maritime Support

Maritime support is provided by the joint force maritime component commander, the Navy component commander, and/or the Marine Corps component commander. Maritime support includes fire support, seabasing operations, deception, and deterrence. Maritime support, such as SOF helicopters landing on Navy ships, typically requires advanced planning and coordination because of technical and safety issues. Additionally, the commander, amphibious task force and the commander, landing force, may also provide amphibious support for the MARSOF and other SOF units. The unique nature of SOF equipment and operational requirements (e.g., communications, weapons, and the need for compartmentalized planning spaces) further reinforce the requirement for early coordination.

For more information on helicopter employment from Navy ships, see JP 3-04, Joint Shipboard Helicopter Operations.

15. Space Support

With the exception of intelligence provided by national technical means, space support for SOF is provided through the USSTRATCOM Joint Functional Component Command for Space upon request by the supported CCDR.

a. For theater level support, Services assign space operators to various joint and Service echelons. JFCs may assign space experts to the joint component commanders' staffs. JFCs and their components request space services and capabilities early in the planning process to ensure effective and efficient use of space assets. Each GCC has a network of space technicians and subject matter expert staff officers, resident on staffs at multiple echelons, who serve as theater advisors for space capabilities (national, military, civil, commercial, and foreign). These individuals concentrate primarily on working the detailed activities of theater space operations based on coordination with the JFC's space coordinating authority in developing, collecting, and prioritizing space requirements. Several DOD and national agencies deploy theater support teams that can provide additional space services and capabilities.

b. Space support personnel can assist SOF commanders and staff in understanding the capabilities, limitations, and effective application of space systems, and ensure that SOF support requirements are clearly understood. Space based support to SOF can include: precision navigation and/or geopositioning, global communications, global intelligence collection, surveillance and warning, meteorological support, imagery for geospatial support and targeting, blue force tracking data, and denying adversary use of space-based capabilities (see Figure IV-3). Satellite threat advisories can provide additional mission security by influencing SOF operational timing.

For further information on space support, refer to JP 3-14, Space Operations, and JP 3-05.1, Joint Special Operations Task Force Operations.

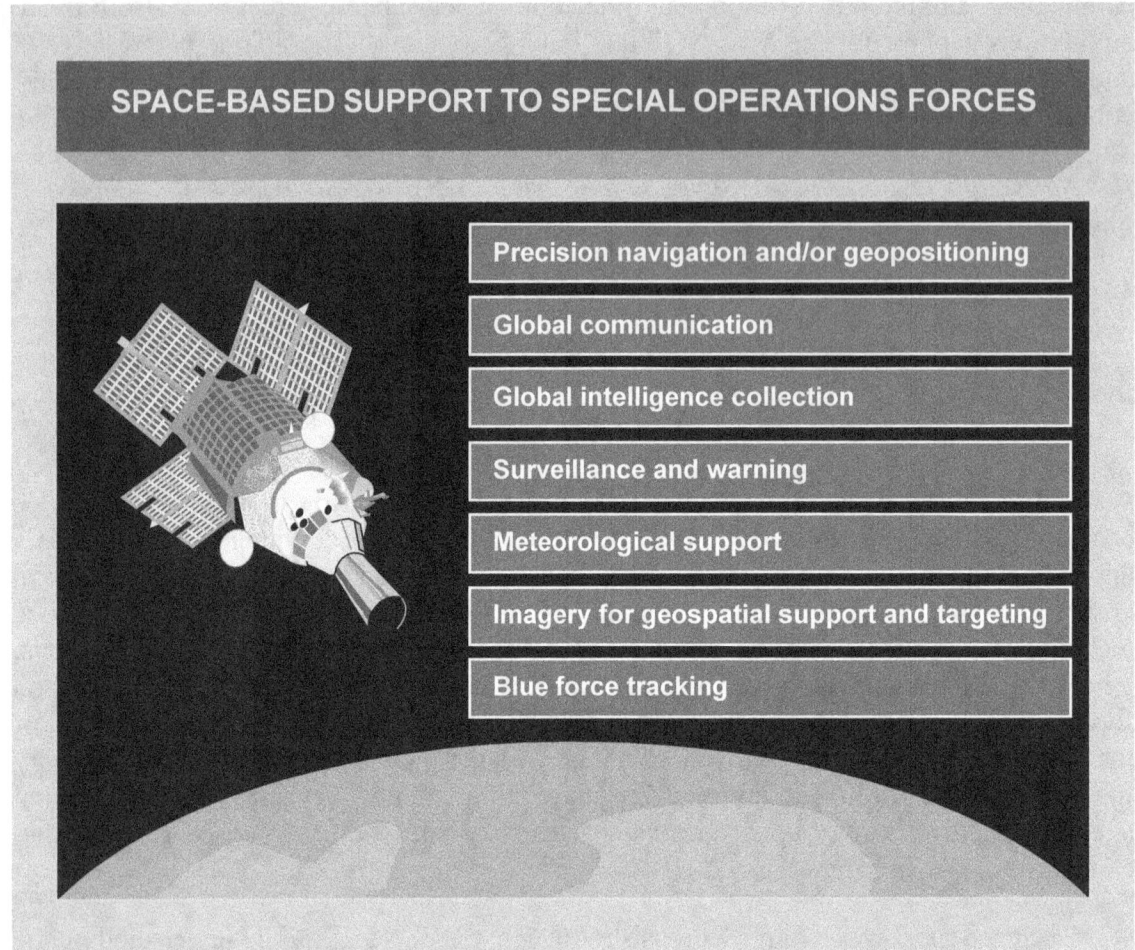

SPACE-BASED SUPPORT TO SPECIAL OPERATIONS FORCES

Precision navigation and/or geopositioning

Global communication

Global intelligence collection

Surveillance and warning

Meteorological support

Imagery for geospatial support and targeting

Blue force tracking

Figure IV-3. Space-Based Support to Special Operations Forces

16. Meteorological and Oceanographic Support

a. **Use of Environmental Data.** Environmental information should be integrated in the SOF commander's decision-making process from initial planning to execution (e.g., joint operational planning process and intelligence preparation of the battlespace). Meteorological and oceanographic (METOC) data can provide information such as studies of general climatology, operational climatology, hydrography, and specific weather forecasts such as mission execution forecast for the operational area focused on operationally significant METOC thresholds. This information can be used by the commander to choose the best windows of opportunity to execute, support, and sustain specific SOF operations.

b. **Exploitation of METOC Conditions.** Potentially, an execution decision may be based on exploiting certain weather and METOC conditions to provide the best advantages in conducting operations while avoiding environmental conditions that will adversely impact operations. SOF units train to exploit every advantage, and operating at the limits of their capabilities, frequently require extraordinarily precise, fine-scale METOC products.

c. **Environmental Effects on Space Operations.** With increased military reliance on space capabilities, the SOF commander must also be kept informed of environmental effects on space operations. METOC support personnel can provide information that will allow the SOF commander to plan for the possibility of the loss of one or more critical space-based systems, such as precision navigation, timing, and communications systems.

For further information on METOC support, refer to JP 3-59, Meteorological and Oceanographic Operations, *and JP 3-05.1,* Joint Special Operations Task Force Operations.

17. Cyberspace Support

Cyberspace crosses all the physical domains and provides military advantage to both SOF and adversaries alike. Cyberspace operations in support of SO can often be conducted remotely, thus reducing the SOF footprint and contributing to freedom of action within a given operational area. The Services maintain cyberspace forces, some of whom are dedicated to providing specific support to SOF. In some cases, those forces are apportioned to SOF directly, while in others, they are simply aligned in a supporting role to SOF.

18. Information Operations Support

IO are integral to successful military operations and especially when conducting SO. The full impact of IO on friendly, neutral, and hostile forces should be considered in the communication strategy of the supported JFC with the goal of achieving and maintaining information superiority for joint and friendly forces. IO are described as the integrated employment of the core capabilities of EW, CNO, MISO, MILDEC, and OPSEC, in concert with specified supporting and related capabilities to influence, disrupt, corrupt, or usurp adversary human and automated decision making while protecting our own.

a. **IO is a SOF core activity, and also integral to the successful execution of many SO.** MISO is a SOF core activity and a core IO capability, as is the IO related capability of CMO, often involved with CA operations, another SOF core activity. SO may require support from any combination of core, supporting, or related IO capabilities, so the JFC's IO cell should include a SOF representative. SOF require IO support, whether SOF are employed independently or in conjunction with CF.

(1) OPSEC and MILDEC are key parts of setting the conditions for operational success of SO. These efforts are central to achieving surprise, helping to isolate the target area, and will also be important enablers for gaining control of the operational environment and neutralizing enemy forces.

(a) OPSEC attempts to deny critical information about friendly forces to the adversary. SOF preparing for deployment can have distinct signatures. Masking the movement of forces to staging bases and to the operational area is essential. These movements may not be totally hidden; however, such detail as the composition of the forces or the time and location of the deployment or infiltration should be concealed. The object is to surprise, confuse, or paralyze the enemy. OPSEC procedures must be planned, practiced, and enforced during training, movement, and operations.

For further details on OPSEC, refer to JP 3-13.3, Operations Security.

(b) MILDEC misleads the adversary as to friendly military capabilities, intentions, and operations, thereby causing the adversary to take specific actions (or inactions) that may contribute to the accomplishment of the friendly mission. MILDEC operations must be closely coordinated with the overall operational scheme of maneuver and other IO efforts. The deception operation will have little effect if it is compromised by poor OPSEC or conflicts with concurrent MISO. Successful military deceptions require sufficient resources, leadership, and linked objectives and goals from the strategic to tactical level.

For further details on MILDEC, refer to JP 3-13.4, Military Deception.

(2) EW includes any military action involving the use of electromagnetic and directed energy to control the electromagnetic spectrum or to attack the enemy. The JFC's plan must be developed to ensure complementary use of assets and weapons systems to effectively disrupt and/or destroy enemy C2 and weapons systems, while protecting joint force capabilities.

See JP 3-13.1, Electronic Warfare, *for additional detail on EW.*

(3) CNO stems from the use of networked computers and supporting information technology infrastructure systems by military and civilian organizations. CNO are cyberspace operations that may very easily be used in support of SO. CNO, along with EW, is used to attack, deceive, degrade, disrupt, deny, exploit, and defend electronic information and infrastructure. For the purpose of military operations, CNO are divided into computer network attack (CNA), CND, and related computer network exploitation (CNE) enabling operations. CNA consists of actions taken through the use of computer networks to disrupt, deny, degrade, or destroy information resident in computers and computer networks, or the computers and networks themselves. CND involves actions taken through the use of computer networks to protect, monitor, analyze, detect, and respond to unauthorized activity within DOD information systems and computer networks. CND actions not only protect DOD systems from an external adversary but also from exploitation from within, and are now a necessary function in all military operations. CNE is enabling operations and intelligence collection capabilities conducted through the use of computer networks to gather data from target or adversary automated information systems or networks. However, it must be understood that many irregular adversaries use the Internet as a means of C2 and for planning purposes, so for example, one form of CNO (e.g., CNE) may be possible when another (e.g., CNA) would not.

b. A goal of a JFC is to shape the information environment to achieve information superiority. The JFC should strive to create and/or sustain desired and measurable effects on foreign TAs; while protecting and defending the JFC's own forces, actions, information, and information systems. As part of IO, the JFC ensures SOF IO requirements are worked into the overall IO planning and execution. SO planning should include considerations for IO support based on the communication strategy of the supported JFC.

c. IO capabilities will also play an integral role in isolating a SO target, whether that isolation is from nearby enemy military forces, or from enemy C2 nodes and centers, both inside and outside the operational area. For example, synchronized CNO and EW, supported by physical attack on a C2 network, could play a decisive role in this isolation.

d. Supporting IO capabilities (IA, physical security, physical attack, counterintelligence, and combat camera) have military purposes other than IO, but they either operate in the information environment or have impact on the information environment.

e. **Related Information Operations Capabilities**

(1) **Defense support to public diplomacy (DSPD)** consists of activities and measures taken by DOD components, not solely in the area of IO, to support and facilitate public diplomacy efforts of the USG. DSPD requires coordination among interagency partners and should be part of the JFC's communication strategy.

(2) **PA** activities are separate, but not isolated from IO. Planning for SO, both by the JFC and SOF, should include PA considerations based on the desired and actual effects of the SO. PA planning should anticipate the potential detection by the enemy and the media of all military operations, with the possible exception of small covert operations. Likewise, PA planning should anticipate potential responses to an unsuccessful operation or adverse effects such as collateral damage.

(3) Properly executed **CMO** in an operational area can reduce potential friction points between the civilian population and the joint force, specifically by minimizing civilian interference with military operations and limiting the impact of military operations on the populace. CMO encompass the activities taken by a commander to establish and maintain effective relations between military forces and civil authorities, the general population, and other civil institutions in friendly, neutral, or hostile areas where those forces are employed. CA forces and units are specifically organized, trained, and equipped to conduct CA operations in support of CMO.

For further details on CMO, refer to JP 3-57, Civil-Military Operations.

19. **Multinational Support**

Multinational support to SOF complements HNS and depends on mission and capability requirements.

a. Support may range from broad assistance to highly structured and integrated support from multinational CF and multinational SOF. Common examples include information and intelligence sharing; providing liaison teams and support to planning efforts; materiel assistance; basing, access, and overflight permission; humanitarian assistance; and linguists and cultural advice and awareness. Multinational CF and multinational SOF have proven invaluable in aiding and augmenting troop rotation, supporting strategic movement, providing medical evacuation, conducting FID, and participating in multinational support teams.

b. Planners must anticipate requirements and prepare for multinational support SOF, sometimes years in advance and on a recurring basis. Various means of preparation include establishment of HQ multinational coordination cells; establishment and use of senior national representatives and defense attachés; specialized predeployment/interoperability training; various agreements (e.g., communications security and cross servicing agreements); and combined training and exercises. In some cases, a joint exchange combined training program might be used to share skills and improve operational capabilities between US and HN forces.

APPENDIX A
REFERENCES

The development of JP 3-05 is based upon the following primary references.

1. General

a. Title 10, USC, as amended.

b. *Unified Command Plan.*

2. Department of Defense

a. DOD Directive 5100.1, *Functions of the Department of Defense and its Major Components.*

b. Department of Defense Instruction 6000.11, *Patient Movement.*

3. Chairman of the Joint Chiefs of Staff

a. Chairman of the Joint Chiefs of Staff Instruction (CJCSI) 3110.01G, *Joint Strategic Capabilities Plan (JSCP).*

b. CJCSI 3110.05D, *Joint Psychological Operations Supplement to the JSCP.*

c. CJCSI 3110.06, *Special Operations Supplemental to JSCP.*

d. CJCSI 3110.12D, *Civil Affairs Supplement to the JSCP.*

e. CJCSI 3210.01A, *Joint Information Warfare Policy.*

f. CJCSI 3214.01, *Military Support to Foreign Consequence Management Operations.*

g. Joint Chiefs of Staff Memorandum 71-87, *Mission and Functions of the US Special Operations Command.*

h. JP 1, *Doctrine for the Armed Forces of the United States.*

i. JP 1-02, *Department of Defense Dictionary of Military and Associated Terms.*

j. JP 1-04, *Legal Support to Military Operations.*

k. JP 2-0, *Joint Intelligence.*

l. JP 2-01, *Joint and National Intelligence Support to Military Operations.*

m. JP 2-01.3, *Joint Intelligence Preparation of the Operational Environment.*

n. JP 2-03, *Geospatial Intelligence Support to Joint Operations.*

o. JP 3-0, *Joint Operations.*

p. JP 3-05.1, *Joint Special Operations Task Force Operations.*

q. JP 3-07.2, *Antiterrorism.*

r. JP 3-07.3, *Peace Operations.*

s. JP 3-07.4, *Joint Counterdrug Operations.*

t. JP 3-08, *Interorganizational Coordination During Joint Operations.*

u. JP 3-09, *Joint Fire Support.*

v. JP 3-13, *Information Operations.*

w. JP 3-13.1, *Electronic Warfare.*

x. JP 3-13.2, *Military Information Support Operations.*

y. JP 3-13.3, *Operations Security.*

z. JP 3-13.4, *Military Deception.*

aa. JP 3-14, *Space Operations.*

bb. JP 3-22, *Foreign Internal Defense.*

cc. JP 3-24, *Counterinsurgency Operations.*

dd. JP 3-26, *Counterterrorism.*

ee. JP 3-29, *Foreign Humanitarian Assistance.*

ff. JP 3-33, *Joint Task Force Headquarters.*

gg. JP 3-40, *Combating Weapons of Mass Destruction.*

hh. JP 3-50, *Personnel Recovery.*

ii. JP 3-57, *Civil-Military Operations.*

jj. JP 3-59, *Meteorological and Oceanographic Operations.*

kk. JP 3-61, *Public Affairs.*

ll. JP 4-0, *Joint Logistics.*

mm. JP 4-02, *Health Service Support.*

nn. JP 4-10, *Operational Contract Support.*

oo. JP 5-0, *Joint Operation Planning.*

pp. JP 6-0, *Communications System Support.*

4. United States Special Operations Command and Service Publications

a. US Army Field Manual 3-05, *Army Special Operations Forces.*

b. US Air Force Doctrine Document 3-05, *Special Operations.*

c. USSOCOM Publication 1, *Special Operations.*

d. USSOCOM Publication 3-11, *Multiservice Tactics, Techniques, and Procedures for Special Operations Forces in Nuclear, Biological, and Chemical Environments.*

e. USSOCOM Document 525-7, *Special Operations Liaison Element (SOLE).*

Intentionally Blank

APPENDIX B
ADMINISTRATIVE INSTRUCTIONS

1. User Comments

Users in the field are highly encouraged to submit comments on this publication to: Commander, United States Joint Forces Command, Joint Warfighting Center Code JW100, 116 Lake View Parkway, Suffolk, VA 23435-2697. These comments should address content (accuracy, usefulness, consistency, and organization), writing, and appearance.

2. Authorship

The lead agent for this publication is the United States Special Operations Command. The Joint Staff doctrine sponsor for this publication is the Director for Operations (J-3).

3. Supersession

This publication supersedes JP 3-05, 17 December 2003, *Doctrine for Joint Special Operations*.

4. Change Recommendations

a. Recommendations for urgent changes to this publication should be submitted:

TO: CDRUSSOCOM MACDILL AFB FL//SOOP-PJ-D//
INFO: JOINT STAFF WASHINGTON DC//J7-JDETD//
           CDRUSJFCOM SUFFOLK VA//JW100//

Routine changes should be submitted to the Director for Joint Force Development (J-7), JDETD, 7000 Joint Staff Pentagon, Washington, DC 20318-7000, with info copies to the USJFCOM JWFC.

b. When a Joint Staff directorate submits a proposal to the Chairman of the Joint Chiefs of Staff that would change source document information reflected in this publication, that directorate will include a proposed change to this publication as an enclosure to its proposal. The Military Services and other organizations are requested to notify the Director, J-7, Joint Staff, when changes to source documents reflected in this publication are initiated.

c. Record of Changes:

CHANGE NUMBER	COPY NUMBER	DATE OF CHANGE	DATE ENTERED	POSTED BY	REMARKS

5. Distribution of Publications

Local reproduction is authorized and access to unclassified publications is unrestricted. However, access to and reproduction authorization for classified JPs must be in accordance with DOD 5200.1-R, *Information Security Program.*

6. Distribution of Electronic Publications

a. Joint Staff J-7 will not print copies of JPs for distribution. Electronic versions are available on the Joint Doctrine, Education, and Training Electronic Information System at https://jdeis.js.mil (NIPRNET), and https://jdeis.js.smil.mil (SIPRNET) and on the JEL at http://www.dtic.mil/doctrine (NIPRNET).

b. Only approved JPs and joint test publications are releasable outside the combatant commands, Services, and Joint Staff. Release of any classified JP to foreign governments or foreign nationals must be requested through the local embassy (Defense Attaché Office) to DIA, Defense Foreign Liaison/IE-3, 200 MacDill Blvd., Bolling AFB, Washington, DC 20340-5100.

c. CD-ROM. Upon request of a joint doctrine development community member, the Joint Staff/J-7 will produce and deliver one CD-ROM with current JPs.

GLOSSARY
PART I—ABBREVIATIONS AND ACRONYMS

AE	aeromedical evacuation
AFSOC	Air Force special operations component
AFSOD	Air Force special operations detachment
AFSOE	Air Force special operations element
AFSOF	Air Force special operations forces
AOI	area of interest
AOR	area of responsibility
ARSOC	Army special operations component
ARSOF	Army special operations forces
ASOC	air support operations center
C2	command and control
CA	civil affairs
CAISE	civil authority information support element
CAO	civil affairs operations
CAP	crisis action planning
CASEVAC	casualty evacuation
CBRN	chemical, biological, radiological, and nuclear
CbT	combating terrorism
CCDR	combatant commander
CDRJSOTF	commander, joint special operations task force
CDRTSOC	commander, theater special operations command
CDRUSSOCOM	Commander, United States Special Operations Command
CF	conventional forces
CJCSI	Chairman of the Joint Chiefs of Staff instruction
CJTF	commander, joint task force
CMO	civil-military operations
CNA	computer network attack
CND	computer network defense
CNE	computer network exploitation
CNO	computer network operations
COA	course of action
COCOM	combatant command (command authority)
COIN	counterinsurgency
COM	chief of mission
CP	counterproliferation
CT	counterterrorism
DA	direct action
DIOCC	Defense Intelligence Operations Coordination Center
DJTFAC	deployable joint task force augmentation cell
DOD	Department of Defense

DOS	Department of State
DSPD	defense support to public diplomacy
EW	electronic warfare
FID	foreign internal defense
FSF	foreign security forces
GCC	geographic combatant commander
GCTN	global combating terrorism network
GEOINT	geospatial intelligence
HN	host nation
HNS	host-nation support
HQ	headquarters
IA	information assurance
IDAD	internal defense and development
IGO	intergovernmental organization
IO	information operations
ISB	intermediate staging base
IW	irregular warfare
JAOC	joint air operations center
JCMOTF	joint civil-military operations task force
JFACC	joint force air component commander
JFC	joint force commander
JFSOC	joint force special operations component
JFSOCC	joint force special operations component commander
JIOC	joint intelligence operations center
JIPOE	joint intelligence preparation of the operational environment
JMISC	Joint Military Information Support Command
JMISOTF	joint military information support operations task force
JP	joint publication
JSOA	joint special operations area
JSOAC	joint special operations air component
JSOACC	joint special operations air component commander
JSOTF	joint special operations task force
JTAC	joint terminal attack controller
JTF	joint task force
LNO	liaison officer
MARSOC	Marine Corps special operations command
MARSOF	Marine Corps special operations forces

METOC	meteorological and oceanographic
MILDEC	military deception
MISO	military information support operations
MNF	multinational force
NAVSOC	Navy special operations component
NAVSOF	Navy special operations forces
NGO	nongovernmental organization
NICC	National Intelligence Coordination Center
NSWTF	naval special warfare task force
NSWTG	naval special warfare task group
OGA	other government agency
OPCON	operational control
OPSEC	operations security
PA	public affairs
PN	partner nation
RC	Reserve Component
RFI	request for information
ROE	rules of engagement
SecDef	Secretary of Defense
SF	special forces
SFA	security force assistance
SO	special operations
SOA	special operations aviation (Army)
SOC	special operations component
SOCCE	special operations command and control element
SOF	special operations forces
SOJTF	special operations joint task force
SOLE	special operations liaison element
SO-peculiar	special operations-peculiar
SOTF	special operations task force
SR	special reconnaissance
SSR	security sector reform
TA	target audience
TACON	tactical control
TACP	tactical air control party
TSOC	theater special operations command
USC	United States Code
USG	United States Government
USJFCOM	United States Joint Forces Command

USSOCOM	United States Special Operations Command
USSTRATCOM	United States Strategic Command
UW	unconventional warfare
WMD	weapons of mass destruction

aeromedical evacuation. The movement of patients under medical supervision to and between medical treatment facilities by air transportation. Also called **AE.** (JP 1-02. SOURCE: JP 4-02)

Air Force special operations base. None. (Approved for removal from JP 1-02.)

Air Force special operations detachment. A squadron-size headquarters that could be a composite organization composed of different Air Force special operations assets, normally subordinate to an Air Force special operations component. Also called **AFSOD.** (Approved for incorporation into JP 1-02.)

Air Force special operations element. None. (Approved for removal from JP 1-02.)

Air Force special operations forces. Those Active and Reserve Component Air Force forces designated by the Secretary of Defense that are specifically organized, trained, and equipped to conduct and support special operations. Also called **AFSOF.** (JP 1-02. SOURCE: JP 3-05)

architecture. None. (Approved for removal from JP 1-02.)

area assessment. None. (Approved for removal from JP 1-02.)

area oriented. None. (Approved for removal from JP 1-02.)

armed reconnaissance. None. (Approved for removal from JP 1-02.)

Army special operations forces. Those Active and Reserve Component Army forces designated by the Secretary of Defense that are specifically organized, trained, and equipped to conduct and support special operations. Also called **ARSOF.** (JP 1-02. SOURCE: JP 3-05)

beach landing site. None. (Approved for removal from JP 1-02.)

blocking position. None. (Approved for removal from JP 1-02.)

bridgehead. None. (Approved for removal from JP 1-02.)

campaign plan. A joint operation plan for a series of related major operations aimed at achieving strategic or operational objectives within a given time and space. (JP 1-02. SOURCE: JP 5-0)

casualty evacuation. The unregulated movement of casualties that can include movement both to and between medical treatment facilities. Also called **CASEVAC.** (JP 1-02. SOURCE: JP 4-02)

center of gravity. The source of power that provides moral or physical strength, freedom of action, or will to act. Also called **COG.** (JP 1-02. SOURCE: JP 3-0)

civil administration. An administration established by a foreign government in (1) friendly territory, under an agreement with the government of the area concerned, to exercise certain authority normally the function of the local government; or (2) hostile territory, occupied by United States forces, where a foreign government exercises executive, legislative, and judicial authority until an indigenous civil government can be established. Also called **CA.** (JP 1-02. SOURCE: JP 3-05)

civil affairs. Designated Active and Reserve Component forces and units organized, trained, and equipped specifically to conduct civil affairs operations and to support civil-military operations. Also called **CA.** (JP 1-02. SOURCE: JP 3-57)

civil affairs operations. Those military operations conducted by civil affairs forces that (1) enhance the relationship between military forces and civil authorities in localities where military forces are present; (2) require coordination with other interagency organizations, intergovernmental organizations, nongovernmental organizations, indigenous populations and institutions, and the private sector; and (3) involve application of functional specialty skills that normally are the responsibility of civil government to enhance the conduct of civil-military operations. Also called **CAO.** (JP 1-02. SOURCE: JP 3-57)

civil-military operations. The activities of a commander that establish, maintain, influence, or exploit relations between military forces, governmental and nongovernmental civilian organizations and authorities, and the civilian populace in a friendly, neutral, or hostile operational area in order to facilitate military operations, to consolidate and achieve operational US objectives. Civil-military operations may include performance by military forces of activities and functions normally the responsibility of the local, regional, or national government. These activities may occur prior to, during, or subsequent to other military actions. They may also occur, if directed, in the absence of other military operations. Civil-military operations may be performed by designated civil affairs, by other military forces, or by a combination of civil affairs and other forces. Also called **CMO.** (JP 1-02. SOURCE: JP 3-57)

combatant command (command authority). Nontransferable command authority established by Title 10 ("Armed Forces"), United States Code, Section 164, exercised only by commanders of unified or specified combatant commands unless otherwise directed by the President or the Secretary of Defense. Combatant command (command authority) cannot be delegated and is the authority of a combatant commander to perform those functions of command over assigned forces involving organizing and employing commands and forces, assigning tasks, designating objectives, and giving authoritative direction over all aspects of military operations, joint training, and logistics necessary to accomplish the missions assigned to the command. Combatant command (command authority) should be exercised through the commanders of subordinate organizations. Normally this authority is exercised through subordinate joint force commanders and Service and/or functional component commanders. Combatant command (command authority) provides full authority to organize and employ commands and forces as the combatant commander considers necessary to accomplish assigned missions. Operational control is inherent in combatant command (command authority). Also called **COCOM.** (JP 1-02. SOURCE: JP 1)

combating terrorism. Actions, including antiterrorism and counterterrorism, taken to oppose terrorism throughout the entire threat spectrum. Also called **CbT.** (JP 1-02. SOURCE: JP 3-26)

combined joint special operations task force. None. (Approved for removal from JP 1-02.)

conventional forces. 1. Those forces capable of conducting operations using nonnuclear weapons. 2. Those forces other than designated special operations forces. Also called **CF.** (JP 1-02. SOURCE: JP 3-05)

counterinsurgency. Comprehensive civilian and military efforts taken to defeat an insurgency and to address any core grievances. Also called **COIN.** (JP 1-02. SOURCE: JP 3-24)

counterterrorism. Actions taken directly against terrorist networks and indirectly to influence and render global and regional environments inhospitable to terrorist networks. Also called **CT.** (JP 1-02. SOURCE: JP 3-26)

covert operation. An operation that is so planned and executed as to conceal the identity of or permit plausible denial by the sponsor. (Approved for incorporation into JP 1-02.)

cutout. None. (Approved for removal from JP 1-02.)

deception. Those measures designed to mislead the enemy by manipulation, distortion, or falsification of evidence to induce the enemy to react in a manner prejudicial to the enemy's interests. (JP 1-02. SOURCE: JP 3-13.4)

denied area. An area under enemy or unfriendly control in which friendly forces cannot expect to operate successfully within existing operational constraints and force capabilities. (JP 1-02. SOURCE: JP 3-05)

direct action. Short-duration strikes and other small-scale offensive actions conducted as a special operation in hostile, denied, or diplomatically sensitive environments and which employ specialized military capabilities to seize, destroy, capture, exploit, recover, or damage designated targets. Also called **DA.** (Approved for incorporation into JP 1-02.)

foreign internal defense. Participation by civilian and military agencies of a government in any of the action programs taken by another government or other designated organization to free and protect its society from subversion, lawlessness, insurgency, terrorism, and other threats to its security. Also called **FID.** (JP 1-02. SOURCE: JP 3-22)

functional component command. A command normally, but not necessarily, composed of forces of two or more Military Departments which may be established across the range of military operations to perform particular operational missions that may be of short duration or may extend over a period of time. (JP 1-02. SOURCE: JP 1)

guerrilla. None. (Approved for removal from JP 1-02.)

guerrilla force. A group of irregular, predominantly indigenous personnel organized along military lines to conduct military and paramilitary operations in enemy-held, hostile, or denied territory. (JP 1-02. SOURCE: JP 3-05)

in extremis. None. (Approved for removal from JP 1-02.)

insurgency. The organized use of subversion and violence by a group or movement that seeks to overthrow or force change of a governing authority. Insurgency can also refer to the group itself. (JP 1-02. SOURCE: JP 3-24)

intelligence preparation of the battlespace. The analytical methodologies employed by the Services or joint force component commands to reduce uncertainties concerning the enemy, environment, time, and terrain. Intelligence preparation of the battlespace supports the individual operations of the joint force component commands. Also called **IPB.** (JP 1-02. SOURCE: JP 2-01.3)

internal defense and development. The full range of measures taken by a nation to promote its growth and to protect itself from subversion, lawlessness, insurgency, terrorism, and other threats to its security. Also called **IDAD.** (JP 1-02. SOURCE: JP 3-22)

irregular forces. Armed individuals or groups who are not members of the regular armed forces, police, or other internal security forces. (JP 1-02. SOURCE: JP 3-24)

joint combined exchange training. A program conducted overseas to fulfill US forces training requirements and at the same time exchange the sharing of skills between US forces and host nation counterparts. Also called **JCET.** (Approved for incorporation into JP 1-02.)

joint force air component commander. The commander within a unified command, subordinate unified command, or joint task force responsible to the establishing commander for making recommendations on the proper employment of assigned, attached, and/or made available for tasking air forces; planning and coordinating air operations; or accomplishing such operational missions as may be assigned. The joint force air component commander is given the authority necessary to accomplish missions and tasks assigned by the establishing commander. Also called **JFACC.** (JP 1-02. SOURCE: JP 3-0)

joint force commander. A general term applied to a combatant commander, subunified commander, or joint task force commander authorized to exercise combatant command (command authority) or operational control over a joint force. Also called **JFC.** (JP 1-02. SOURCE: JP 1)

joint force special operations component commander. The commander within a unified command, subordinate unified command, or joint task force responsible to the establishing commander for making recommendations on the proper employment of assigned, attached, and/or made available for tasking special operations forces and assets; planning and coordinating special operations; or accomplishing such operational missions as may be assigned. The joint force special operations component commander is given the authority necessary to accomplish missions and tasks assigned by the establishing commander. Also called **JFSOCC.** (JP 1-02. SOURCE: JP 3-0)

joint servicing. That function performed by a jointly staffed and financed activity in support of two or more Services. (Approved for incorporation into JP 1-02.)

joint special operations air component commander. The commander within a joint force special operations command responsible for planning and executing joint special operations air activities. Also called **JSOACC.** (JP 1-02. SOURCE: JP 3-05)

joint special operations area. An area of land, sea, and airspace assigned by a joint force commander to the commander of a joint special operations force to conduct special operations activities. It may be limited in size to accommodate a discrete direct action mission or may be extensive enough to allow a continuing broad range of unconventional warfare operations. Also called **JSOA.** (JP 1-02. SOURCE: JP 3-0)

joint special operations task force. A joint task force composed of special operations units from more than one Service, formed to carry out a specific special operation or prosecute special operations in support of a theater campaign or other operations. Also called **JSOTF.** (Approved for incorporation into JP 1-02.)

Marine Corps special operations forces. Those Active Component Marine Corps forces designated by the Secretary of Defense that are specifically organized, trained, and equipped to conduct and support special operations. Also called **MARSOF.** (JP 1-02. SOURCE: JP 3-05.1)

multinational force. A force composed of military elements of nations who have formed an alliance or coalition for some specific purpose. Also called **MNF.** (JP 1-02. SOURCE: JP 1)

multinational operations. A collective term to describe military actions conducted by forces of two or more nations, usually undertaken within the structure of a coalition or alliance. (JP 1-02. SOURCE: JP 3-16)

multinational warfare. None. (Approved for removal from JP 1-02.)

national security. A collective term encompassing both national defense and foreign relations of the United States. Specifically, the condition provided by: a. a military or defense advantage over any foreign nation or group of nations; b. a favorable foreign relations position; or c. a defense posture capable of successfully resisting hostile or destructive action from within or without, overt or covert. (Approved for incorporation into JP 1-02 with JP 1 as the source JP.)

naval mobile environmental team. None. (Approved for removal from JP 1-02.)

naval special warfare. A naval warfare specialty that conducts special operations with an emphasis on maritime, coastal, and riverine environments using small, flexible, mobile units operating under, on, and from the sea. Also called **NSW.** (Approved for incorporation into JP 1-02.)

naval special warfare special operations component. None. (Approved for removal from JP 1-02.)

noncombatant evacuation operations. Operations directed by the Department of State or other appropriate authority, in conjunction with the Department of Defense, whereby noncombatants are evacuated from foreign countries when their lives are endangered by war, civil unrest, or natural disaster to safe havens as designated by the Department of State. Also called **NEOs.** (JP 1-02. SOURCE: JP 3-68)

nongovernmental organization. A private, self-governing, not-for-profit organization dedicated to alleviating human suffering; and/or promoting education, health care, economic development, environmental protection, human rights, and conflict resolution: and/or encouraging the establishment of democratic institutions and civil society. Also called **NGO.** (JP 1-02. SOURCE: JP 3-08)

operational control. Command authority that may be exercised by commanders at any echelon at or below the level of combatant command. Operational control is inherent in combatant command (command authority) and may be delegated within the command. Operational control is the authority to perform those functions of command over subordinate forces involving organizing and employing commands and forces, assigning tasks, designating objectives, and giving authoritative direction necessary to accomplish the mission. Operational control includes authoritative direction over all aspects of military operations and joint training necessary to accomplish missions assigned to the command. Operational control should be exercised through the commanders of subordinate organizations. Normally this authority is exercised through subordinate joint force commanders and Service and/or functional component commanders. Operational control normally provides full authority to organize commands and forces and to employ those forces as the commander in operational control considers necessary to accomplish assigned missions; it does not, in and of itself, include authoritative direction for logistics or matters of administration, discipline, internal organization, or unit training. Also called **OPCON.** (JP 1-02. SOURCE: JP 1)

operational environment. A composite of the conditions, circumstances, and influences that affect the employment of capabilities and bear on the decisions of the commander. Also called **OE.** (JP 1-02. SOURCE: JP 3-0)

operations security. A process of identifying critical information and subsequently analyzing friendly actions attendant to military operations and other activities to: a. identify those actions that can be observed by adversary intelligence systems; b. determine indicators that adversary intelligence systems might obtain that could be interpreted or pieced together to derive critical information in time to be useful to adversaries; and c. select and execute measures that eliminate or reduce to an acceptable level the vulnerabilities of friendly actions to adversary exploitation. Also called **OPSEC.** (JP 1-02. SOURCE: JP 3-13.3)

overt operation. An operation conducted openly, without concealment. (JP 1-02. SOURCE: JP 2-01.2)

paramilitary forces. Forces or groups distinct from the regular armed forces of any country, but resembling them in organization, equipment, training, or mission. (JP 1-02. SOURCE: JP 3-24)

personnel recovery. The sum of military, diplomatic, and civil efforts to prepare for and execute the recovery and reintegration of isolated personnel. Also called **PR.** (JP 1-02. SOURCE: JP 3-50)

preparation of the environment. An umbrella term for operations and activities conducted by selectively trained special operations forces to develop an environment for potential future special operations. Also called **PE.** (Approved for inclusion in JP 1-02.)

Rangers. Rapidly deployable airborne light infantry organized and trained to conduct highly complex joint direct action operations in coordination with or in support of other special operations units of all Services. (Approved for incorporation into JP 1-02.)

resistance movement. An organized effort by some portion of the civil population of a country to resist the legally established government or an occupying power and to disrupt civil order and stability. (Approved for incorporation into JP 1-02 with JP 3-05 as the source JP.)

SEAL delivery vehicle team. United States Navy forces organized, trained, and equipped to conduct special operations with SEAL delivery vehicles, dry deck shelters, and other submersible platforms. (Approved for inclusion in JP 1-02.)

SEAL team. United States Navy forces organized, trained, and equipped to conduct special operations with an emphasis on maritime, coastal, and riverine environments. (Approved for replacement of "sea-air-land team" and its definition in JP 1-02.)

security force assistance. The Department of Defense activities that contribute to unified action by the United States Government to support the development of the capacity and capability of foreign security forces and their supporting institutions. Also called **SFA.** (JP 1-02. SOURCE: JP 3-22)

special activities. None. (Approved for removal from JP 1-02.)

special boat team. United States Navy forces organized, trained, and equipped to conduct or support special operations with combatant craft and other small craft. Also called **SBT.** (Approved for incorporation into JP 1-02.)

special forces. US Army forces organized, trained, and equipped to conduct special operations with an emphasis on unconventional warfare capabilities. Also called **SF.** (JP 1-02. SOURCE: JP 3-05)

special forces group. The largest Army combat element for special operations consisting of command and control, special forces battalions, and a support battalion capable of long duration missions. Also called **SFG.** (Approved for incorporation into JP 1-02.)

special forces operations base. None. (Approved for removal from JP 1-02.)

special operations. Operations requiring unique modes of employment, tactical techniques, equipment and training often conducted in hostile, denied, or politically sensitive environments and characterized by one or more of the following: time sensitive, clandestine, low visibility, conducted with and/or through indigenous forces, requiring regional expertise, and/or a high degree of risk. Also called **SO.** (Approved for incorporation into JP 1-02.)

special operations command. A subordinate unified or other joint command established by a joint force commander to plan, coordinate, conduct and support joint special operations within the joint force commander's assigned operational area. Also called **SOC.** (JP 1-02. SOURCE: JP 3-05)

special operations command and control element. A special operations element that is the focal point for the synchronization of special operations forces activities with conventional forces activities. Also called **SOCCE.** (Approved for incorporation into JP 1-02.)

special operations forces. Those Active and Reserve Component forces of the Military Services designated by the Secretary of Defense and specifically organized, trained, and equipped to conduct and support special operations. Also called **SOF.** (JP 1-02. SOURCE: JP 3-05.1)

special operations liaison element. A special operations liaison team provided by the joint force special operations component commander to the joint force air component commander (if designated), or appropriate Service component air command and control organization, to coordinate, deconflict, and integrate special operations air, surface, and subsurface operations with conventional air operations. Also called **SOLE.** (JP 1-02. SOURCE: JP 3-05)

special operations-peculiar. Equipment, material, supplies, and services required for special operations missions for which there is no Service-common requirement. Also called **SO-peculiar.** (Approved for incorporation into JP 1-02.)

special operations weather team. A task organized team of Air Force personnel organized, trained, and equipped to collect critical environmental information from data sparse areas. Also called **SOWT.** (Approved for replacement of "special operations weather team/tactical element" and its definition in JP 1-02.)

special reconnaissance. Reconnaissance and surveillance actions conducted as a special operation in hostile, denied, or politically sensitive environments to collect or verify information of strategic or operational significance, employing military capabilities not normally found in conventional forces. Also called **SR.** (Approved for incorporation into JP 1-02.)

special tactics. None. (Approved for removal from JP 1-02.)

special tactics team. An Air Force task-organized element of special tactics that may include combat control, pararescue, tactical air control party, and special operations weather personnel. Also called **STT.** (Approved for incorporation into JP 1-02.)

subordinate unified command. A command established by commanders of unified commands, when so authorized by the Secretary of Defense through the Chairman of the Joint Chiefs of Staff, to conduct operations on a continuing basis in accordance with the criteria set forth for unified commands. A subordinate unified command may be established on an area or functional basis. Commanders of subordinate unified commands have functions and responsibilities similar to those of the commanders of unified commands and exercise operational control of assigned commands and forces within the assigned operational area. Also called subunified command. (JP 1-02. SOURCE: JP 1)

subversion. Actions designed to undermine the military, economic, psychological, or political strength or morale of a governing authority. (JP 1-02. SOURCE: JP 3-24)

tactical control. Command authority over assigned or attached forces or commands, or military capability or forces made available for tasking, that is limited to the detailed direction and control of movements or maneuvers within the operational area necessary to accomplish missions or tasks assigned. Tactical control is inherent in operational control. Tactical control may be delegated to, and exercised at any level at or below the level of combatant command. Tactical control provides sufficient authority for controlling and directing the application of force or tactical use of combat support assets within the assigned mission or task. Also called **TACON.** (JP 1-02. SOURCE: JP 1)

task-organizing. None. (Approved for removal from JP 1-02.)

terrorism. The unlawful use of violence or threat of violence to instill fear and coerce governments or societies. Terrorism is often motivated by religious, political, or other ideological beliefs and committed in the pursuit of goals that are usually political. (JP 1-02. SOURCE: JP 3-07.2)

theater special operations command. A subordinate unified command established by a combatant commander to plan, coordinate, conduct, and support joint special operations. Also called **TSOC.** (Approved for incorporation into JP 1-02.)

unconventional warfare. Activities conducted to enable a resistance movement or insurgency to coerce, disrupt, or overthrow a government or occupying power by operating through or with an underground, auxiliary, and guerrilla force in a denied area. Also called **UW.** (Approved for incorporation into JP 1-02.)

weapons of mass destruction. Chemical, biological, radiological, or nuclear weapons capable of a high order of destruction or causing mass casualties and exclude the means of transporting or propelling the weapon where such means is a separable and divisible part from the weapon. Also called **WMD.** (JP 1-02. SOURCE: JP 3-40)

JOINT DOCTRINE PUBLICATIONS HIERARCHY

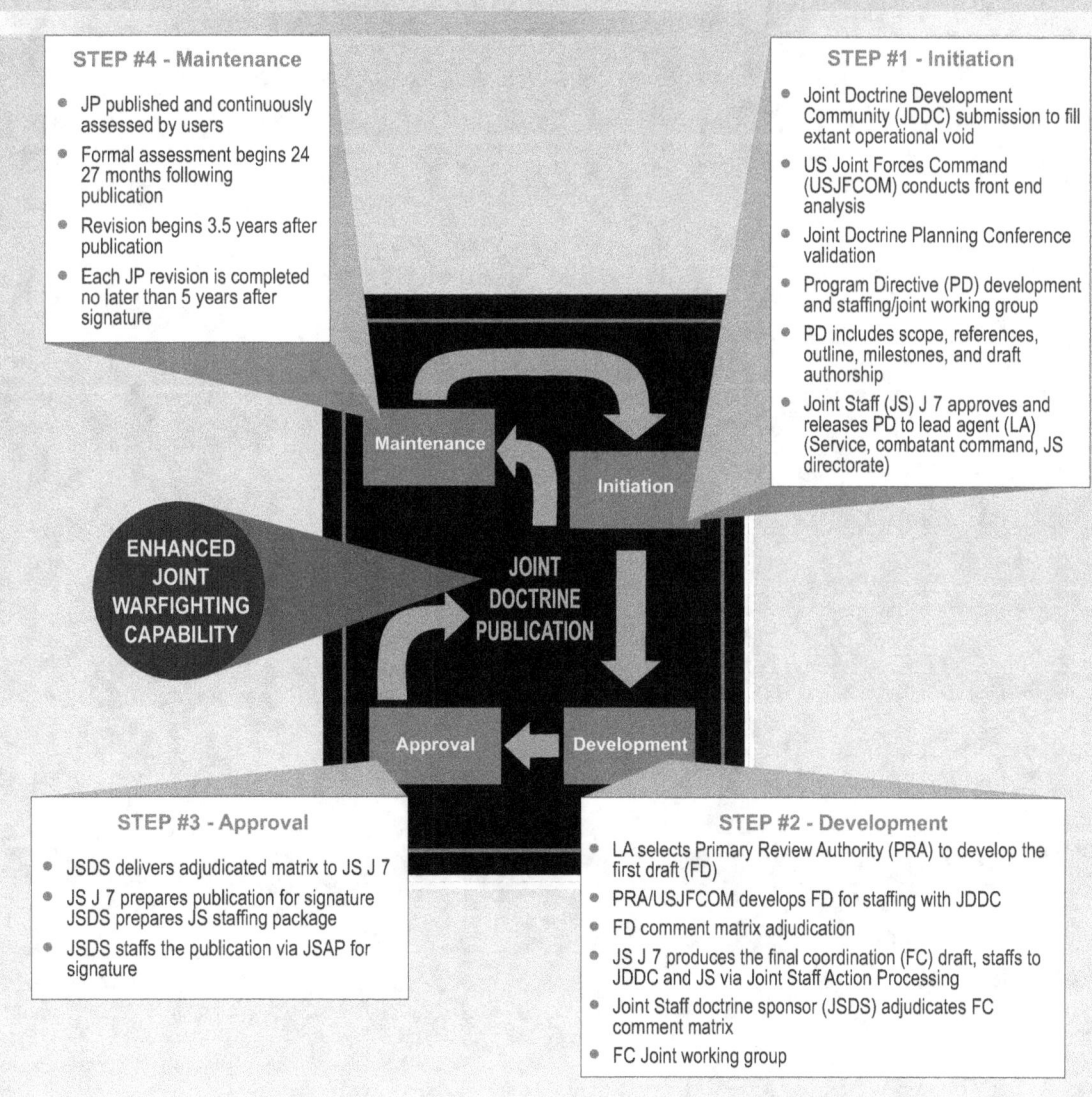

```
                            ┌──────────────┐
                            │     JP 1     │
                            │    JOINT     │
                            │   DOCTRINE   │
                            └──────────────┘
```

JP 1-0	JP 2-0	JP 3-0	JP 4-0	JP 5-0	JP 6-0
PERSONNEL	INTELLIGENCE	OPERATIONS	LOGISTICS	PLANS	COMMUNICATIONS SYSTEM

All joint publications are organized into a comprehensive hierarchy as shown in the chart above. **Joint Publication (JP) 3-05** is in the **Operations** series of joint doctrine publications. The diagram below illustrates an overview of the development process:

STEP #4 - Maintenance

- JP published and continuously assessed by users
- Formal assessment begins 24-27 months following publication
- Revision begins 3.5 years after publication
- Each JP revision is completed no later than 5 years after signature

STEP #1 - Initiation

- Joint Doctrine Development Community (JDDC) submission to fill extant operational void
- US Joint Forces Command (USJFCOM) conducts front end analysis
- Joint Doctrine Planning Conference validation
- Program Directive (PD) development and staffing/joint working group
- PD includes scope, references, outline, milestones, and draft authorship
- Joint Staff (JS) J 7 approves and releases PD to lead agent (LA) (Service, combatant command, JS directorate)

ENHANCED JOINT WARFIGHTING CAPABILITY

JOINT DOCTRINE PUBLICATION

Maintenance — Initiation — Approval — Development

STEP #3 - Approval

- JSDS delivers adjudicated matrix to JS J 7
- JS J 7 prepares publication for signature JSDS prepares JS staffing package
- JSDS staffs the publication via JSAP for signature

STEP #2 - Development

- LA selects Primary Review Authority (PRA) to develop the first draft (FD)
- PRA/USJFCOM develops FD for staffing with JDDC
- FD comment matrix adjudication
- JS J 7 produces the final coordination (FC) draft, staffs to JDDC and JS via Joint Staff Action Processing
- Joint Staff doctrine sponsor (JSDS) adjudicates FC comment matrix
- FC Joint working group